DE PROPRIETATIBUS LITTERARUM

edenda curat

C. H. VAN SCHOONEVELD

Indiana University

Series Maior, 28

TYPOLOGY
AND
SEVENTEENTH-CENTURY
LITERATURE

by

JOSEPH A. GALDON, S.J.

Ateneo de Manila University

1975

MOUTON

THE HAGUE · PARIS

ISBN 90 279 3151 8

Printed in The Netherlands by Mouton & Co., The Hague

PREFACE

Several studies in recent years have discovered the richness of theological and religious themes in seventeenth-century literature. In *The Elizabethan World Picture*, E. M. W. Tillyard says of the seventeenth century: "One can say dogmatically that it was solidly theocentric and that it was a simplified version of a much more complicated medieval picture." Louis Martz has studied the meditative tradition, and there have been many investigations into the influence of the Bible and theology on many of the seventeenth-century writers. But there is one particular area of biblical influence that has been largely neglected in seventeenth-century studies until recent years, and that is the impact of biblical typology on the literature of the age. In an article on the figurative interpretation in Milton, H. R. MacCallum remarks that "Little has yet been done to apply the discoveries made by these scholars [on Typology] to Renaissance and Reformation literature". Northrop Frye, William Madsen, and Rosemond Tuve, especially, have made contributions in this area in recent years, but a considerable amount of work still remains to be done.

I do not think that the importance of this influence can be over-estimated. For biblical typology is more than simply biblical exegesis, a method of interpreting scripture which relates persons and events as type and anti-type, shadows and fulfillments of each other. It represents, in a broader sense, a world view, a way of looking at persons and events in the light of a theology of history which postulates the presence and the relevance of an eternal God at every individual moment of time.

Biblical typology and this world view of biblical history are as characteristic and pertinent in the seventeenth century as E. M. W. Tillyard's five other 'world views' — order, sin, the chain of being, corresponding planes and the cosmic dance. Biblical typology is reflected in the literature of the seventeenth century to a far greater degree and, I feel, with more specific detail than the meditative tradition discussed by Professor

Martz. It is as pervasive an influence as the rhetorical tradition and the poetics of Rosemund Tuve and Ruth Wallerstein.

I am aware that the theological and scriptural dimensions of typology are far more complicated than may appear from the first part of the present discussion. But my emphasis has been largely literary, and I have been content with a rather minimal discussion of the more technical aspects of typology. My exposition has admittedly oversimplified many of the theological and scriptural aspects, and I have deliberately avoided many points of dispute, for example, the discussion of the *sensus plenior*, and the relationship of the typological interpretation to the medieval four senses of scripture. This latter point is discussed very briefly in the Appendix. My purpose in the first part of this study has been to provide an explanation of typology in terms that would be understood by the non-theologian, and which would be useful for a deeper appreciation of typological themes in seventeenth-century literature.

The second part of this study which applies this notion of typology to literary themes, is obviously far from comprehensive. The application of typological images in seventeenth-century literature offers almost un-limited possibilities. My intention has been merely to provide indications of some few typological themes as a means of illustrating the use of these concepts by the writers of the period. There is considerable area here for further investigation into the use of typology by individual authors, and its occurrence in individual works. As our awareness of the biblical and typological background of the seventeenth century increases, so will our appreciation of the literature of the age.

I am grateful to Professors Marjorie H. Nicolson, Edward W. Tayler, and Joseph A. Mazzeo, all of Columbia University, who have guided my work in Seventeenth-Century Literature. Professor Nicolson first encouraged me in investigating the use of theological and biblical images in the poets of the century, and Professor Tayler was most helpful and enthusiastic when I first broached the possibility of the present book. His own interest in the subject has encouraged me at every stage of the present work. I am grateful to Professor Philip Calderone, S.J., of the Ateneo de Manila University, for his suggestions and criticism of the sections on the theory of typology and to the Ateneo de Manila University for a Research Grant which made the publication of this work possible.

It is needless to say that I am deeply indebted to Professor Mazzeo's own work on typology in Dante and the seventeenth century, and that without his help and direction the work would not have reached its present form. His own conviction of the value of the great humanistic traditions, both scriptural and classical, in the literature of the seventeenth century has been a constant source of inspiration.

Joseph A. Galdon, S.J.
Ateneo de Manila University
Quezon City, Philippines

TABLE OF CONTENTS

I

THE SEVENTEENTH-CENTURY TYPOLOGICAL WORLD VIEW

> There is need of the scholar's ability to live with these
> ancient thinkers, enter into their categories, speak their
> language.
>
> De Lubac, *Exégèse Mediévale*, p. 11.

It is a truism to say that no age is a simple age. All ages are complicated, and it is not at all untrue to say that every age really is an age of contrasts. It is unfortunate that every analysis of a period in history must of necessity oversimplify. Every anatomy of an age, in a sense, destroys the age, for it is impossible to anatomize a living thing.

The seventeenth century is no exception to this rule. Critical works, unfortunately, especially critical studies of the literature of the period, have tended to oversimplify, and at the same time, paradoxically, to overcategorize. In the discovery of the relevance of the great chain of being, the planes of correspondence, the scientific revolution, the meditative or rhetorical traditions, for example, other equally valid elements in the structure of a very complicated age may tend to be overlooked. The seventeenth century, like all ages, had *many* ways of looking at the world, and no one world view is really exclusive of the others. But, at the root and basis of all other world views, there was no doubt in the minds of the seventeenth-century citizens that God existed and providentially directed the world. This Divine Relevance is fundamental in any approach to the seventeenth century, and it is this pertinence of the divine which makes the great chain of being, the meditative tradition or the planes of correspondence, even the scientific revolution, viable for the seventeenth century.

Any reader familiar with the seventeenth century is aware of the fact that the period was an extremely religious age. A brief glance at the *Short-Title Catalogue* of Pollard and Redgrave or Wing will indicate the large number of religious works in the literature of the period.[1]

[1] A. W. Pollard and G. R. Redgrave, *A Short-Title Catalogue of Books Printed in*

Douglas Bush reports that more than two-fifths of the books printed in England from 1480 to 1640 were religious, and the percentage is still higher for the years 1600-1640.

In Jaggard's Catalogue of 1619 nearly three-fourths of the books are religious and moral; in William London's Catalogue of the Most Vendible books in England (1657-1658) the space given to works of divinity equals that occupied by all other kinds together. ... Grotius and Casaubon declared, in the middle of James' reign, that there was little or no literary scholarship in England, that theology was the only interest of educated men.[2]

In the year 1620, one hundred and thirty books were entered at Stationer's Hall, London, and of that number, more than half were religious in subject matter — sermons, scriptural exegesis, religious controversy, sacred verse, prayers, etc.[3] In the seventeenth century, religious literature, far from being the very specialized interest of just a few, was of vital concern to the specialist and to the general reading public as well. Milton's *Paradise Lost*, the great religious classic of the century, is just one of many examples. Browne, Donne, and Dryden are others. The men of the seventeenth century devoted a great deal of time and effort to what would be considered rather esoteric studies in scripture and theology, and this interest in religious literature was not limited to a select few, but was widespread among even the common readers of the period.

Fundamental, and indeed essential, to all this religious thought and writing was the Bible. There can be no doubt that the Bible was the most widely read of all books in the period. There are almost 1000 references to the Bible in Pollard and Redgrave and almost 700 more in Wing. The Bible was a book that was not only read, but was known and used, and the scriptural concept of man and the world exerted a deep and lasting influence even on the ordinary laymen of the period. For it is important to remember that education and culture in the seventeenth century were still almost entirely ecclesiastical and religious. Milton's early years at

---

England, Scotland and Ireland and of English Books Printed Abroad, 1475-1640 (London: Bibliographical Society, 1946); Donald Wing, *A Short-Title Catalogue of Books Printed in England, Scotland, Ireland, Wales and British America and of English Books Printed in Other Countries, 1641-1700*, 3 vols. (New York: Columbia University Press, 1945).
[2]   Douglas Bush, *English Literature in the Earlier Seventeenth Century*, 2nd ed. rev. (Oxford: Clarendon Press, 1962), 310. See the whole of Chapter X on Religion and Religious Thought, and the sections on the Bible (65 ff.) for further evidence of the prevailing interest in religion in the period. Also *The Cambridge History of the Bible: The West From the Reformation to the Present Day*, ed. S. L. Greenslade (Cambridge University Press, 1963).
[3]   Helen C. White, *Devotional Literature (Prose) 1600-1640* (Madison, Wisconsin: University of Wisconsin Press, 1931), 11.

St. Paul's were strongly influenced by the Bible and biblical history. The three great languages of every educated man were still Greek and Latin and the scriptural Hebrew. A schoolboy's earliest exercises, as were Milton's, were likely to be paraphrases on the Psalms or other biblical passages.[4]

Sermons are another indication of the place of the Bible in the seventeenth century. It is difficult for us to realize the importance of the preached sermon in the period. As Bush remarks: "It is hardly possible to exaggerate the importance of the sermon in the seventeenth-century world", and he quotes Evelyn, who wrote: "The religion of England is preaching and sitting still on Sundaies."[5]

The seventeenth century in England was *par excellence* an age of sermons. It was a century of violent theological and political upheaval, and the sermons of the period reflect its varying opinions and emotions as no other literary remains of the time can be said to do; for the sermon, except in a few cases ... was a public pronouncement of the views held by an appreciable number of contemporary Englishmen. ... For one person who witnessed a play or ten who happened to read it, thousands may, without exaggeration, be said to have attended sermons or afterwards studied them from shorthand notes or in printed copies.[6]

Almost without exception, these sermons were expositions of biblical terms, and rich in quotations from the Bible. All of Donne's sermons are expositions of biblical texts, and Walton tells us that Donne began preparing his sermons by searching for a biblical text:

... for as he usually preached once a week, if not oftener, so after his sermon he never gave his eyes rest, till he had chosen out a new text, and that night cast his sermon into form, and his text into divisions; and the next day he took himself to consult the Fathers ...[7]

[4] See Donald Leman Clark, *John Milton at St. Paul's School* (New York: Columbia University Press, 1948), 100-130 where the course of studies at St. Paul's is discussed, and also Harris Francis Fletcher, *The Intellectual Development of John Milton*, 2 vols. (Urbana: University of Illinois Press, 1956, 1961), especially Chapter V of Volume II on religious instruction and knowledge of the Bible.

[5] Douglas Bush, *English Literature in the Earlier Seventeenth Century*, 312.

[6] W. Fraser Mitchell, *English Pulpit Oratory from Andrewes to Tillotson* (London: SPCK, 1932), 3-4. See also Arnold Williams, *The Common Expositor* (Chapel Hill: University of North Carolina Press, 1948), 37-38.

[7] Isaak Walton, *Lives of John Donne, Sir Henry Wotton, Richard Hooker, George Herbert and Robert Sanderson* (London: Oxford University Press, 1962), 67. For further indication of the prevalence of biblical influences, one need only glance at the numerous biblical quotations and references in these lives of Walton, originally published in 1640, 1651, 1655 and 1670. See also Don C. Allen, "Dean Donne Sets His Text", *Journal of English Literary History*, X (1934), 208-229 and Dennis B. Quinn, "John Donne's Principles of Biblical Exegesis", *Journal of English and German Philology*, LXVI (April, 1962), 313-329.

Francis Bacon, who should certainly not be suspected of any excessive religious enthusiasm, as White points out,[8] in his survey of the state of knowledge in his own time, speaks with respect and appreciation of the distinction which contemporary English preachers had achieved in the field of biblical comment and interpretation.[9]

A final indication of the prevalence of biblical knowledge among the common people of the seventeenth century can be found in the devotional books of the period. Helen White has studied these devotional works in some detail, and she points out that a great number of them were Psalters or Primers, books which dealt with versions of the Psalms, adapted for daily reading and prayer. She also emphasizes the importance of scripture in all of these devotional works which enjoyed such a great popularity among the ordinary readers of the period.[10]

It is difficult to assess the actual impact of the Bible on the seventeenth century. Bush speaks of:

... the "noblest monument of English prose", the great moulder of English literature and life, the Bible unofficially authorized by King James in 1611. ... But to attempt here a formal discussion of the religious and literary influence of the Bible, as of the book itself, would be predestinate absurdity — *Si monumentum requiris, circumspice.*[11]

It is obvious that men of the seventeenth century read the Bible. It is equally obvious that they read the Bible in a special way, for the seventeenth-century reader invariably read the Bible typologically. He was still closely connected with the continuous tradition of biblical exegesis that went back to the early Christians who interpreted the events of Christ's life in terms of the Old Testament. The world of the scriptures was still familiar to the seventeenth-century reader and it was natural for him to attempt to express his own experiences in terms borrowed from the Old and the New Testaments. He was accustomed to hearing from the pulpit

---

[8]   White, *Devotional Literature (Prose) 1600-1640*, 10.
[9]   Francis Bacon, *The Advancement of Learning*, ed. William Aldis Wright (Oxford, 1900), 264, or in the Everyman Edition (London: J. M. Dent and Sons, 1930), 215-219.
[10]   Helen C. White, *The Tudor Books of Private Devotion* (Madison, Wisconsin: University of Wisconsin Press, 1951), esp. Chapter III on the Psalter, and Chapter IX on Scripture for Private Devotion.
[11]   Bush, *English Literature in the Earlier Seventeenth Century*, 65, 66, 72. See also the following: "It is difficult for a secular age to comprehend the importance of the Book of Genesis, or of the Bible as a whole, in the culture of the Renaissance. However much the men of the sixteenth and seventeenth centuries may have looked to Greece and Rome for the patterns and materials of their intellectual life, they were primarily Christians, and their habit of mind was predominantly theological." — Williams, *The Common Expositor*, 3.

and in school the traditional typological interpretations of the scripture. He would be familiar with the typological references to the Patriarchs and their wives in the Marriage ceremony from the Book of Common Prayer,[12] and he would often have heard the prayer from the ceremony for the Public Administration of Baptism:

Let us Pray: Almighty and everlasting God, which of thy great mercy didst save Noe and his family in the ark, from perishing by water: and also didst safely lead the children of Israel, thy people, through the Red Sea; figuring thereby thy holy Baptism ... we beseech thee, for thy infinite mercies, that thou wilt mercifully look upon these children, sanctify them, and wash them with thy Holy Ghost; that they, being delivered from thy wrath, may be received into the Ark of Christ's Church ...[13]

Steeped in this typological way of thinking and looking at scripture, the seventeenth-century reader would naturally have read the story of Isaac in terms of Christ's sacrifice on the cross. The Exodus would have carried a clear message for him of both Christ's passage from the dead, and the individual Christian's passage from sin to life again. He would have been accustomed to seeing Noah, Moses or Joseph as types of Christ. Many events of the Old Testament would have been significant for him not only in terms of their actual reality, but as foreshadowings and prefigurations of those greater things to come. He would have discovered a continuing pattern of God's providence running through both the Old and the New Testaments, and reaching even unto his own particular case. He would have appreciated and listened with perfect understanding to Sandys' Christmas Sermon:

His birth, foreshadowed so long ago by the heavenly prophet, was in fulness of time accomplished, as this day in Bethlehem, a city of David, according to the testimony of that angel sent from heaven to proclaim the birth of the Son of God at the same time saying: "Behold I bring you tidings of great joy, that shall be unto all the people; because this day is born unto you a Saviour, which is Christ Our Lord in the city of David." This is that seed of the woman which breaketh the serpent's head, that meek Abel murdered by his brother for our sin, that true Isaac whom his father hath offered up to be sacrifice of pacification and atonement between him and us. This is that Melchisedech, both a King and a Priest that liveth forever, without father or mother, beginning or ending. This is that Joseph that was sold for thirty pieces of silver. This is that Samson

[12] *The Book of Common Prayer and Administration of the Sacraments and Other Rites and Ceremonies of the Church of England* (London, 1559), in: *Liturgy and Occasional Forms of Prayer Set Forth in the Reign of Queen Elizabeth*, edited for the Parker Society by Rev. William Keating Clay (Cambridge: At the University Press, 1847), 217ff.
[13] *The Book of Common Prayer*, 200.

full of strength and courage, who to save his people and destroy his enemies hath brought death upon his own head. ... This is that Bridegroom in the canticle. ... This is that Lamb of God, pointed at by John. ... This is the child that is born for us.[14]

The seventeenth-century reader would have understood perfectly when Lancelot Andrewes prayed: "The Typical Lamb. Behold!"[15]

There was a basis for this typological view of the Bible, in the Gospels themselves and in St. Paul. Christ himself had used this typological mode of thinking, linking the Old and the New Testaments, in his explanation of the text of Isaiah 41:1-2 in the synagogue at Nazareth: "This day this text is fulfilled in your hearing."[16] Again, with the disciples on the road to Emmaus, He explained the words used of himself in all the scriptures, beginning with Moses and the Prophets.[17] Matthew was profoundly convinced of the relationship between the two testaments, and he realized that the details of Christ's life were actual fulfillments of Old Testament events which foreshadowed the historical details of Christ's coming. Matthew was writing for the Jewish community, and this typological approach would have made complete sense to them, steeped as they were in the Old Testament writings.[18]

Typology is also the implicit foundation of John's account of the final week of Christ's life and his account of the Last Supper and the Passion. For John, Christ is the New Pasch, the Lamb of God. Typology is at the basis of most of Paul's theologizing. The stereotyped phrases, "It is written", "As Isaiah says", "In order that it might be accomplished", etc., appear more than 200 times in the New Testament text and 118 times in St. Paul.[19]

It is clear that the authors of the New Testament, just as the Jews of

---

[14]   *Sermons* made by the most reverend Father in God, Edwin, Archbishop of York, Primate of England and Metropolitan at London (London, 1585), edited for the Parker Society by Rev. John Ayre (Cambridge: At the University Press, 1841), 7-8.

[15]   Lancelot Andrewes, *The Private Devotions*, ed. Thomas S. Kepler (Cleveland-New York: The World Publishing Company, 1956), 156. For a summary of this typological outlook, see G. W. H. Lampe, "The Reasonableness of Typology", *Essays in Typology* (Naperville, Illinois: Alec R. Allenson, Inc., 1957), 9–12.

[16]   Luke 4:22.

[17]   Luke 24:27.

[18]   John J. O'Rourke, "The Fulfillment Texts in Matthew", *Catholic Biblical Quarterly* XXIV (October, 1962), 394-403. O'Rourke has studied these fulfillment texts in Matthew in great detail, with their accompanying references to Old Testament texts.

[19]   L. Venard, "Utilization de l'Ancien Testament dans le Nouveau", *Initiation Biblique*, ed. A. Robert and A. Tricot (Paris: Desclee et Cie, 1954), 446. For an excellent and profoundly scholarly summary of Paul's use of the Old Testament, see E. Earle Ellis, *Paul's Use of the Old Testament* (Edinburgh: Oliver and Boyd, 1957).

their own time, firmly believed in the existence in the scriptures of a sense
more meaningful than the merely literal sense. Because of this spiritual
sense, the events and personages of Jewish history became, above and
beyond their own historical reality, types and figures of spiritual realities
still to come and to be accomplished in the historical context of the New
Testament. This was the tradition which stood behind the reading and
the understanding of the Bible in the seventeenth century, as well as in
all ages which preceded it. It was a tradition of typological, figural
interpretation which had come down through the Fathers of the Church —
Augustine, Tertullian, Origen, Jerome and Ambrose — who were almost
as popular as the Bible itself in the seventeenth century.[20]

The typological interpretation of scripture was as meaningful to the
seventeenth-century reader as the scientific or psychiatric categories are
to us in our time. Because our contemporary world has largely lost this
sense of the Bible, it comes as an alien and a stranger to this biblical and
typological world view which was so much a part of the life of the
seventeenth century. James H. Sims laments:

... the growing ignorance and lack of interest in the doctrines and even the once-
familiar stories of the Bible. In an age when not a single member of a graduate
class in English at a major state university can identify Keats' allusion to Ruth's
standing "in tears amid the alien corn" and when only a handful of students in
a large freshman class can recognize the story of the Prodigal Son when it is
read to them from a modern English translation, there is not much hope that a
poet who depends on a general sensitivity to Biblical allusions on the part of the
literate public will be very popular reading even in academic circles.[21]

A good deal of this seventeenth-century typological world view has also
been lost in the past three hundred years. The ordinary reader or listener
in the seventeenth century would have been perfectly at home in the
midst of allusions to type and anti-type, to shadows and figures. Take for
example a passage like the following from Donne's Sermon preached to
the King at Whitehall on the First Sunday of Lent, February 11, 1626–
1627:

Peace is in Sion; God's whole quire is in tune; Nay here is the Musick of the
sphears; all the Sphears (all Churches), all the stars in those Sphears (all
Expositours in all Churches), agree in the sense of these words, and agree the
words to be a Prophesie, of the Distillation, nay Inundation, of the largeness,

[20]   See Ruth Wallerstein, *Studies in Seventeenth Century Poetic* (Madison, Wisconsin:
University of Wisconsin Press, 1950), 188.
[21]   James H. Sims, *The Bible in Milton's Epics* (Gainesville: University of Florida
Press, 1962), 1-2.

nay the infinitenesse of the blessings and benefits of Almighty God, prepared and meditated before, and presented and accomplished now in the Christian Church. The sun was up betimes, in the light of nature, but then the Sun moved but in the winter Tropick, short and cold, dark and cloudy days; a Diluculum and a Crepusculum, a Dawning and a Twilight, a little traditionall knowledge for the past, a little conjucturall knowledge for the future made up their day. The Sunne was advanced higher to the Jews in their Law; but then the Sunne was but in Libra; as much day as night; there was as much Baptisme, as Circumcision in that Sacrament; and as much Lamb as Christ; their Law was their Equinoctiall, in which they might see both the Type, and that which was figured in the Type; but in the Christian Church the Sun is in a perpetuall Summer Solstice; which are high degrees, and yet there is a higher, the Sun is in a perpetuall Meridian and Noon, in that summer Solstice. There is not only a *surge* Sol but a *siste* Sol: God hath brought the sun to the height, and fixt the sun in that height in the Christian Church where he in his own sonne by his Spirit hath promised to dwell *usque ad consummationem*, till the end of the world. Here is Manna; and not in Gomers, but in barns; and Quails; and not in Heaps, but in Hills; the waters above the firmament, and not in drops of dew, but in showers of former and latter rain; and the land of Canaan; not in Paradise onely, nor onely in performance and possession, but in Extension and Dilatation.[22]

The passage can be properly understood only in the context of a typological interpretation of scripture, a context which was clearly a part of the seventeenth-century world view and the equipment of almost every seventeenth-century citizen on the street.

[22]   John Donne, *The Sermons*, ed. George R. Potter and Evelyn M. Simpson (Berkeley and Los Angeles: University of California Press, 1953), VII, 349-350. See also *The Sermons of John Donne*, selected and edited by Theodore A. Gill (New York: Meridian Books, Inc., 1958), 203-204.

II

THE DEFINITION OF TYPOLOGY

> Opera loquuntur ... Facta, si intelligas, verba sunt.
> Augustine, *Sermo* 95:3.

In classical Greek, the word τύπος is derived from the root τύπτειν which means 'to strike', and it has the basic meaning of a 'blow' or the 'mark' or 'imprint' left by a blow.[1] Its most common and frequent meaning is the 'impression' made on wax by a seal, and the majority of its other meanings are derived from this one basic meaning. These other meanings of τύπος can generally be classified under the heading of 'mold', the pattern from which the seal impressions are made, or under the heading of the 'impression' or 'image' produced by the mold. Other meanings, such as 'form', 'shape', 'general impression', and 'outline' may refer either to the mold or to the impression, or to both.[2]

The biblical uses of the word τύπος correspond to these two main headings of model or pattern and image. In Acts 7:43–44, for example, the word occurs in each sense, and the references are to Amos 5:26 and Exodus 25:40, which are the only two places where the word occurs in the Old Testament. In Romans 6:17 and Philippians 3:17, the word means a pattern or a model. Romans 5:14 and I Corinthians 10:6 are the first uses of τύπος in a strictly theological context and the word again means pattern or model. In Romans 5:14, Adam is called a τύπος, a pattern or model for Christ.[3]

---

[1] For the general outline of these remarks on the lexicography of the word τύπος, see K. J. Woollcombe, "The Biblical Origins and Patristic Development of Typology", *Essays On Typology* (Naperville, Ill.: Alec R. Allenson, Inc., 1957), 60-65, and "Le Sens de 'Type' Chez les Pères", *La Vie Spirituelle*, Supplement, IV (Février, 1951), 84-100. For a similar study of the history and use of the Latin word *Figura*, cf. Erich Auerbach, "Figura", *Scenes From the Drama of European Literature* (New York: Meridian Books, Inc., 1959), 11-78. This article is translated by Ralph Manheim from the original German text in *Neue Dantestudien* (Istanbul, 1944), 11-71. The same article occurs with minor changes in *Archivum Romanicum*, XXII (1938), 436-489.

[2] Cf. Liddell and Scott, s.v. τύπος.

[3] Nygren, A., "Commentary on Romans", *ET*, 219, cited by Woollcombe, "Biblical Origins and Patristic Development of Typology", 69.

It is important to note that the word τύπος is ambiguous. It may mean either the pattern or the impression, either the original or the copy. The word ἀντίτυπος is also therefore ambivalent. This explains why Adam is sometimes called a type of Christ, at other times an antitype, and Baptism is either a type or an antitype of the flood. Τύπος may either be the primary concept or the secondary image,[4] but in typological exegesis, the 'type' is usually applied to the Old Testament 'shadow' and the 'antitype' to the New Testament fulfillment.

In a *Homily on the Passion* in the second century, Melito of Sardis illustrates most clearly the connection between the root meaning of the word τύπος and the typological method of scriptural exegesis. In that sermon, Melito compares the Old Testament types to the scale models which a sculptor uses as patterns or models while he is working on the full scale statue. The model is of use only while the statue is being made. By looking at the model, the sculptor can form a mental picture of the finished statue and he knows how to shape his material accordingly. But when the statue is finished, he discards the model because it is no longer of any use. In exactly the same way Melito says:

The People was held in honor before the Church arose, and the Law was wondrous before the light of the Gospel was shed abroad. But since the Church arose and the Gospel was shed abroad upon men on earth, the type is made void, giving over the image to the natural truth.[5]

Melito then goes on to show how the Old Passover must be discarded, because in Christ, the Paschal Lamb of God, the type has been fulfilled and the model is no longer necessary.

Melito's analogy was later used by both Origen and Chrysostom. Origen wrote:

Just as those artists who make images out of bronze and mold statues first make a clay model of the finished product before they make the actual statue out of bronze or silver or gold ... so you must understand that the same thing is true in those things which are written or occur as types or figures of future events in the Law and the Prophets.[6]

[4] See, for example, the Greek text of the New Testament, John 20:25, Acts 7:43-44, Romans 6:17, Philippians 3:17, Romans 5:14, 1 Corinthians 10:6, 11, where the word appears in both senses.
[5] Melito of Sardis, *Homily on the Passion*, edited by Campbell Bonner in *Studies and Documents*, ed. Kirsopp Lake and Silva Lake (London: 1940), XII, p. 107. See also the definitive text and the French translation in *Papyrus Bodmer* XIII, Meliton de Sardis, *Homilie sur la Pâque* (Bibliotheca Bodmeriana, 1960).
[6] *Hom.* 10:1 in *Lev.*

Chrysostom changes the image slightly and speaks of the outline or preliminary sketch which a painter makes for a portrait before he fills in the colors.[7] But the basic notion remains the same in both images. The type is a model, a pattern which is fulfilled and perfected in the completed work of art, the antitype. It is this basic meaning of type and antitype, as pattern and impression, which is at the basis of all scriptural typology.

In any biblical passage, there are, first and foremost, the literal words of the text. As St. Thomas points out, the function of the words in the biblical text is the same as in any other book. They are the signs of things, they signify realities other than themselves. This significance of the literal words must be gathered from the text itself and from the context. But the Bible is a unique book. Because God governs the whole of history, the realities, the *res ipsae* of the biblical text have a divine reference to other events of history. As Augustine says: "We must look for the mystery in the deed itself, not only in the words."[8] St. Thomas sums this all up in the *Summa*:

God, the author of Holy Scriptures, has power to give meaning, not only to words (men can do this), but also to things. Thus (in the Bible) as in all fields of knowledge words have meaning, but here also the very objects which words signify also have a particular meaning of their own. The first meaning whereby words signify things is their literal or historical sense. The meaning whereby the things signified by the words signify other things is said to be their spiritual sense, which is based upon the literal sense and supposes it.[9]

In God's book, the words speak as in any other volume, but because it is God's book, not only the words but also the persons and events of the biblical history have tongues as well and they speak as loudly as the words themselves. As Augustine says: "Opera loquuntur ... Facta, si intelligas, verba sunt."[10]

The Jews of the Old Testament, God's Chosen People, are liberated from captivity in Egypt, they pass through the waters of the Red Sea, and

---

[7] *Hom.* 10:2 in *Phil.*
[8] "In ipso facto, non solum in dicto, mysterium requirere debemus." — *In Ps.* 68:2:6, *PL* 36:858.
[9] "Dicendum quod auctor Sacrae Scripturae est Deus, in cujus potestate est ut non solum voces ad significandum accommodet, quod etiam homo potest facere, sed etiam res ipsas. Et ideo, cum in omnibus scientiis voces significent, hoc habet proprium ista scientia quod ipsae res significatae per voces etiam significant aliquid. Illa ergo prima significatio, qua voces significant res, pertinet ad primum sensum, qui est sensus historicus vel litteralis. Illa vero significatio qua res significatae per voces iterum res alias significant dicitur sensus spiritualis qui super litteralem fundatur et eum supponit." — *Summa Theol.*, 1:1:10. In this passage, Aquinas depends heavily upon Augustine, *De Trin.*, 3, *PL* 46:1068. See also Aquinas, *Quodlibet*, 7, a.14.
[10] Augustine, *Sermo*, 95:3, *PL* 35:582.

after years of wandering and hardship in the desert, they come to the
Promised Land. This is more than just a word. It is also a historical fact.
Yet while it remains fully and completely a historical event in its own
right, it is also a sign, a type of other realities — of Christ's liberation
from the dead, of the individual soul's liberation from the captivity of sin
through the waters of Baptism.

Now these events have become prototypes (τύποι) applicable to ourselves ...
and all these things which happened to our ancestors were typical (τυπικῶς)
events and they have been written down to be a warning to us upon whom the
fullness of time has come.[11]

John Milton uses this same example of the Exodus when he speaks of the
senses of Scripture in the *De Doctrina Christiana.*[12]

Milton's *sensus compositus ex historia et typo* is a clear echo of the
Thomistic and Patristic *sensus litteralis et sensus spiritualis.* John Donne
echoes the Thomistic passage even more clearly in the *Devotions*:

My God, My God, thou art a direct God, may I not say a literal God, a God
that wouldst be understood literally and according to the plain sense of all thou
sayest? But thou art also (Lord, I intend it to thy glory, and let no profane
misinterpreter abuse it to thy diminution), thou art a figurative, a metaphorical
God too: a God in whose words there is such a height of figures, such voyages,
such perigrinations to fetch remote and precious metaphors, such extensions,
such spreadings, such curtains of allegories, such third heavens of hyperboles,
so harmonious elocutions, so retired and reserved expressions, so commanding
persuasions, so persuading commandments, such sinews even in thy milk, and
such things in thy words, as all profane authors seem of the seed of the serpent
that creeps, thou art the dove that flies ... Neither art thou a figurative, a
metaphorical God in thy word only, but in thy works too. The style of thy
works, the phrase of thine actions, is metaphorical. The institution of thy
whole worship in the old law was a continual allegory; types and figures overspread all, and figures flowed into figures, and poured themselves out into
further figures: circumcision carried a figure of baptism, and baptism carries a
figure of that purity which we shall have in perfection in the new Jerusalem.[13]

In more technically biblical language elsewhere, Donne approves the
same basic notion of typology:

And as Lyra notes, being perchance too Allegoricall and Typick in this, it hath
this in common with all other books, that the words signifie things; but hath
this particular, that all the things signifie other things.[14]

[11] I Corinthians, 10:6, 11.
[12] Chapter XXX.
[13] John Donne, *Devotions Upon Emergent Occasions* (Ann Arbor, Mich.: Michigan
University Press, 1959), Expostulation, XIX, 124-129.
[14] John Donne, *Essays in Divinity* (ed. Evelyn M. Simpson; Oxford: Clarendon Press,
1952), 8. For Lyra, cf. *Glossa Ordinaria, PL* 113:25.

This Exodus, then, is much more than mere metaphor, much more than just an artificial sign, for it has a reality all its own. It is a thing, a *res* in the Thomistic sense. Yet it is an historical event, a biblical thing, that is also a type of other realities. The thing signifies other things; the realities of Jewish history are an image, a figure of other realities that are still to come.[15]

Typology uncovers this correspondence between the persons, events, and things of the Old Testament and the persons, events, and things of the New Testament. This correspondence is present because God controls the whole of history, and it is God who causes the earlier individuals, groups, and events to embody characteristics which foreshadow later events.[16] Some 'things' about which the text of scripture speaks literally are also used by God to prefigure other things in the future. As Eichrodt points out, there is a homogeneity in God's relation in both the Old and the New Testament, unlike any other religion known in history, and there is a continuing line of 'divine relevance' which moves through the Old and New Testaments and has its ultimate perspective in Jesus Christ who is the fulfillment of the shadows embodied in the literal *res* of the Old Testament. The Old Testament Flood, the Exodus, the Exile, the Return, have a significance in themselves which goes far beyond the literal meaning of the text and embodies a prophetic foreshadowing and reference to other later, and similar events. This is also true of Old Testament personages like Adam, Abraham, Moses, Joshua, David, and of the Old Testament images like King, Prophet, Messiah, Servant, and Son of Man.[17]

Typology may, therefore, be defined as the method of interpreting scripture in which the persons and events, incidents and narratives of the Old Testament, the Old Testament *res ipsae*, are viewed as realities which are also at one and the same time prophetic signs and foreshadowing of the persons and events in God's redemptive plan as it is fulfilled and revealed in the New Testament.

---

[15]   William Lynch, *Christ and Apollo* (Sheed and Ward: New York, 1960). There is also a Mentor-Omega edition (New York: New American Library, 1960), 184-185. See also L. Venard, *Dictionnaire de la Bible*, Supplement II, col. 46: "les réalités de l'histoire juive étaient une image, une symbole, une figure de réalités spirituelles à venir."
[16]   A. Berkeley Mickelson, *Interpreting the Bible* (Grand Rapids, Michigan: Wm. B. Eardman Publishing Co., 1963), 242-243. See also p. 212 where Mickelsen quotes Walter Eichrodt, "Ist die Typologische Exegese sachgemasse Exegese?", *Probleme Altetestamentlicher Hermeneutik* (ed. Claus Westerman; Munchen: Chr. Kaiser Verlag, 1960).
[17]   Alan Richardson, "The Rise of Modern Biblical Scholarship and Recent Discussions of the Authority of the Bible", *Cambridge History of the Bible*, 335-336.

Erich Auerbach's concept of 'Figuralism', although solidly based on biblical typology, is much broader than the notion of strict biblical typology since it encompasses the analogical applications of biblical type to all forms of literature. He maintains that:

... figural interpretation establishes a connection between two events or persons, the first of which signifies not only itself, but the second, while the second encompasses or fulfills the first. The two poles of the figure are separate in time, but both, being real events or figures, are within time, within the stream of historical life.[18]

Thus, an event signifies not only itself, but at the same time it signifies, or relates to another event which it predicts and foreshadows. But it does this without destroying its own reality. The events are strictly literal; they are not abstractions. But figuralism is a spiritual sense, because the understanding of the two events and of the link between them is a spiritual act. The connection is not primarily a chronological or causal connection, but a unity within the divine plan, which is reflected in all earthly events. The direct historical connection between the events is of secondary importance and can often be dispensed with completely in the understanding of the figural or typological link between the events.[19]

The study of typology is complicated by the bewildering variety of terminology, interpretation, and explanation of the senses of scripture in the writings of the Fathers of the Church and the early biblical commentators. Origen speaks of the "vast forests of the Scriptures",[20] but as Danielou points out:

... how much more true is this of the luxuriant growth of commentaries which have grown up round the Scriptures. True enough that attempts have been

---

[18] Auerbach, "Figura", 53-54 and Erich Auerbach, *Mimesis* (Willard Trask, tr.; Princeton: Princeton University Press, 1953), 555, 16-17, 73. This latter work also appears in a Doubleday Anchor Book (New York, 1953). Auerbach has also treated the notion of Figuralism or "phenomenal prophecy", as he sometimes calls it, in other works. Cf. "Figurative Texts Illustrating Certain Passages of Dante's Commedia", *Speculum*, XXI (1946), 474–489. (This is a continuation of the earlier article "Figura", with specific references and examples of figuralism from Dante);"Typological Symbolism in Medieval Literature", *Yale French Studies*, IX (1952), 3-10. This same topic is treated more extensively in *Typologische Motive in der Mittelalterlichen Literatur* (= *Schriften und Vertrage Des Petrarca-Institute Köln*, II) (Krefeld: Scherpe-Verlag, 1953); *Introduction to Romance Language and Literature*, trans. from the French by Guy Daniels (New York: Capricorn Books, 1961).

[19] Woollcombe, "Biblical Origins", 39-40, where a distinction is made between typology as a method of exegesis and typology as a form of writing.

[20] *Hom.* 4:1 in *Ezech.* See also Tyconius, *Lib. Reg.*, quoted by Augustine, *De Doctrina Christiana*, III:30:43, *PL* 34:82.

made to classify. The various senses of Scripture have been grouped together. But these attempts, for want of scientific analysis, have often made matters worse by introducing artificial categories.[21]

It is clear enough that the classical and traditional interpretation of scripture spoke of just two senses — the literal, or carnal sense, of the text, and the spiritual sense. But the spiritual sense, in particular, was referred to under many titles, and because of the ambiguity of these terms — mystical, allegorical, figurative, spiritual — it is extremely difficult if not at times literally impossible to understand what each of the early scriptural writers meant. There is no agreed or generally accepted terminology because the early commentators were not primarily interested in the careful analysis and distinction of the senses of scripture.

... les auteurs du Nouveau Testament, voulant établir cette harmonie préordonnée par Dieu, ne se sont pas soucies des distinctions des théologiens postérieurs, qui ont distingué le sens litteral, des sens typiques, allégoriques, spirituels, etc.[22]

It is even more difficult to precipitate and purify the notion of typology out of the maze of conflicting interpretations and opinions in the early Fathers.

The word τύπος occurs sixteen times in the New Testament, and eleven times in St. Paul, but strangely enough the word allegory (ἀλληγορία) is Paul's most frequent term for the conception of typology, and allegory rather than typology is the word most commonly used by the early Fathers when referring to this method of scriptural interpretation. In his comments on Galations 4:24, Chrysostom says that when Paul uses the word ἀλληγορία, he really means τύπος.[23] It seems clear enough that Paul in this passage (Galatians 4:24) diverted a word (allegoria) from its original meaning because he was confronted with a new concept which had no analogy among the Greeks or even among the Jews. The Latin Fathers, especially, did not distinguish typology from allegory, and often grouped both methods of exegesis under the term 'spiritual interpretation'.[24] St. Thomas uses the term *allegoria* as the general term for 'spirit-

---

[21] Jean Danielou, *From Shadows to Reality*, trans. Dom Wulfstan Hibbard (Westminster, Maryland: Newman Press, 1960), VII.

[22] J. van der Ploeg, O.P., "L'exégèse de l'Ancien Testament dans l'Epître des Hébreux", *Révue Biblique*, LV (1947), 192.

[23] "καταχρηστικῶς τὸν τύπον ἀλληγορίαν ἐκάλεσε." — Gaume, X, 710 b. See also: "Dans les interpretations bibliques de saint Paul, c'est plutôt au sens typique qu'au sens proprement allégorique qu'on a affaire." — L. Venard, "Citations de l'Ancien Testament dans le Nouveau Testament", *Dictionnaire de la Bible, Supplement*, II (1934), col. 49.

[24] *PG* 61:662. For a fuller discussion of Paul's use of the word allegory, cf. Henri de

ual interpretation', with typology as one of the varieties of the spiritual sense.[25] In other places it is obvious that the typical and the allegorical sense are often synonomous for St. Thomas.[26]

The Latin word *figura* is also used synonymously with both type and allegory in the early scriptural commentators and this adds a further complication to the study of the meaning of typology in the Fathers and scriptural exegetes. As has been seen, for example, Erich Auerbach uses the term figuralism practically synonomously with the Patristic notion of typology. Although the word *allegoria* seems to have a broader meaning in the early Fathers, and is apparently used to refer to any deeper meaning in the text (thus coinciding with the spiritual sense), the boundary between type and figure and allegory is very fluid. Tertullian, for example, uses the words *allegoria* and *figura* as synonyms; Origen at times makes no distinction in his use of type and allegory.

Because of the confusion in terminology, the meaning of the words allegory, type, and figure, as well as the use of the spiritual and mystical senses of scripture must be carefully studied in each author. It is unfair to rule out the possible use of the notion of typology in an author just because the word itself does not occur. Danielou, for example, points out that Origen's use of typology is often confused with his use of allegory and his biblical exegesis is often totally rejected on this account. The confusion in Origen is largely due to his apparently confusing terminology.[27] Yet, as Burghardt indicates:

We should realize [that] the term allegory has a legitimate authorized origin in St. Paul; we can support the thesis that, despite a certain amount of inconsistency, Origen uses 'allegory' essentially as the Latin tradition in general and St. Thomas in particular, to designate either the ensemble of exegetical

Lubac, "'Typologie' et 'Allégorisme'", *Recherches de Science Religieuse*, XXXIV (1947), 181ff. For a brief survey of allegory and scriptural interpretation, see Robert McNally, S.J., *The Bible in the Early Middle Ages* (Westminster, Maryland: Newman Press, 1959), 53-61.
[25] "Sed attendendum est, quod allegoria sumitur aliquando pro quolibet mystico intellectu; aliquando pro uno tantum ex quattuor (sensibus) Sacrae Scripturae ... Mysticus autem sensus, seu spiritualis, dividitur in tres. Primo namque, sicut dicit Apostolus, lex vetus est figura novae legis; et ideo, secundum quod ea quae sunt veteris legis significant ea quae sunt novae, est sensus allegoricus." — *Expositio in Ep. ad Gal.*, c. IV, Lect. 7. See also *Summa Theol.*, I; q. 1, a. 10.
[26] "Sic est allegoricus sensus vel typicus, secundum quod ea quae a veteri testamento contigerunt, exponuntur de Christo et ecclesia." — *Quaestiones Quodlibitales*, VII, a. 15.
[27] Jean Danielou, *Origen*, trans. Walter Mitchell (New York: Sheed and Ward, 1955), 174ff. See also de Lubac, "Typologie", 180ff. See, for example, chapters 2 and 3 in the *De Principiis* of Origen, *Origen on First Principles*, trans. G. W. Butterworth (London: SPCK, 1936), 269-312.

approaches which outstrip the letter, or the typical sense as contradistinguished from the historical sense on the one hand and from the spiritual senses (tropology and anagogy) on the other.[28]

This relationship of type and allegory in particular will be discussed in much greater detail in Chapter III, where the two exegetical methods will be clearly distinguished on the basis of the historical realism of the terms of the biblical relationship. Because of this historical confusion in terminology it becomes all the more necessary that typology be clearly defined, and its essential characteristics must be very clearly discussed so as to differentiate it from other similar and sometimes overlapping forms of the spiritual interpretation.

For the temptation to lapse into subjectivism is always present in any approach to typological exegesis. There is a basic unity between the Old Testament and the New Testament, and there certainly is a recurring parallelism of theme and interpretation, but strict typology does not exist everywhere in the Bible, and typological interpretation must be rigidly controlled so that it does not degenerate into mere subjectivism.

There is no evidence that the New Testament writers (with the possible exception of the author of the Apocalypse) were writing cryptograms filled with mysterious images visible only to the eyes of the initiate. The New Testament impresses one as, on the whole, a healthy, open, straightforward document.[29]

This is even more true when typology is applied to literature and biblical images in literature. The great danger is that the reader or critic begins to see types everywhere in literature and to discover typology in every biblical allusion in poetry. But typology is much more than biblical allusion. In the seventeenth century, as in the centuries that preceded it, the Bible played a large and pervasive role in the lives of people, as has been seen in Chapter I on the Seventeenth-Century Typological World View. It was inevitable that this world view would be reflected in the literature of the period. But frequent biblical allusion, even a biblical habit of mind, or way of looking at things, the inevitable result of the emphasis placed on the Bible, is not strict typology. Occasional, fragmentary and merely illustrative use of images derived from the Bible is not typology. One need only page through the *Divine Poems* of John Donne, or the *Paradise Lost* of Milton to discover innumerable biblical allusions and images. But relatively few of these images and allusions are strict types. The chances are that where typology is not explicitly indicat-

[28] Walter J. Burghardt S.J., "On Early Christian Exegesis", *Theological Studies*, XI (March, 1950), 110.
[29] Robert C. Dentan, "Typology — Its Use and Abuse", *Anglican Theological Review*, XXXIV (1952), 215.

ed, or at least obvious and clear to the ordinarily skilled reader once it
has been pointed out, there is no typology at all. The study of typology
especially in its literary manifestations, already one step removed from the
biblical text itself, is a precarious occupation. It requires, and indeed demands, in Woollcombe's terminology, both "attention and precaution".[30]

Father Musurillo points out very clearly the ground rules which should
govern this use of attention and precaution in the study of typology:

... if we are faced with linguistic communication, there should be objective
rules by which the meaning of the text, its precise denotation and connotation,
can be derived. Contrariwise, these rules should be clear enough so that the
critic can say (within reasonable limits) that X is the meaning and that Y is to be
definitely excluded.[31]

It is important to distinguish what Lampe calls "legitimate and exe-
getically justifiable typology" from "the unwarrantable exercise of private
and uncontrolled ingenuity", between types which can be "rationally
explained and defended" and those "which are far-fetched".[32] The
explicit nature of typology should be investigated in some detail, then,
and an attempt should be made to discover working rules that will
eliminate as much as possible the danger of critical subjectivism and
relativism in the study of literary and biblical typology in the seventeenth
century.

Typological exegesis is basically a disciplined theological activity.[33]
It does have determined rules and norms, and typology in the strict
sense includes four essential elements which distinguish and characterize
it as a form of biblical interpretation. These four elements are the
historical realism of both terms of the typological relationship, the type
and the antitype; the basic and essential correspondence between the two
terms, the similarity between the two; the relationship of shadow to reality, the notion that one pole of the typological reference must be a fulfillment, a *forma perfectior*, of the other; and finally, the divine resonance and

---

[30]   Woollcombe, "Le Sens de 'Type' Chez Les Pères", 84.
[31]   Herbert Musurillo, S.J., "Shadow and Reality: Thoughts On The Pattern of Typology", *Theological Studies*, XXII (1961), 458.
[32]   G. W. H. Lampe, "The Reasonableness of Typology", *Essays on Typology* (Naperville, Ill.: Alec R. Allenson, Inc., 1957), 21.
[33]   A. G. Hebert, *The Authority of the Old Testament* (London: Faber and Faber, Ltd.,
1947), 233 and chapter 7, *passim*, where Hebert distinguishes typology as a strict theological activity from what he calls the illustrative use of scripture. For a brief summary
of typological exegesis with relevant bibliography from 1600 to date, cf. Joseph Coppens,
Les Harmonies des Deux Testaments, nouvelle édition revue et augmentée (Tournai-
Paris: Casterman, 1949), 78-82.

Christic correspondence of the type and antitype within the biblical theology of history.[34]

---

[34] For a good summary of the principles of biblical typology, though from a different viewpoint than the one adopted in the following chapters, cf. Lucien Delporte, "Les Principes de la typologie biblique et les éléments figuratifs du Sacrifice de l'Expiation (Lev. 16)", *Ephemerides Theologicae Lovanienses*, III (1926), 307-327.

III

THE ELEMENTS OF TYPOLOGY

> The problem before us is to discover some means of dis-
> tinguishing between helpful and misleading forms of
> typology; we have to try to separate those which can be
> rationally explained and defended from those which are
> farfetched.
> G. W. H. Lampe, "The Reasonableness of Typology", 21.

1. TYPOLOGICAL REALISM

Scriptural scholars have always stressed the fact that typology is solidly
based upon the *things* (*res ipsae*), and not upon the *words* (verba) of
scripture. 'Things' must be understood broadly to include persons and
events. Although some scriptural scholars restrict typology to historical
events, most would concede that even a fictional event (e.g., Jonah in the
whale) may be typological.[1] Although the type signifies the antitype, and
the antitype fulfills the type, this significance and fulfillment which they
embody does not destroy their own reality, but simply adds a deeper
meaning to the persons, places, things or events of the Old Testament
and links them to New Testament persons, places, or events. Auerbach's
figuralistic terminology stresses this realism of typology, for in various
places he speaks of the nature of typology as "figural realism", "phenomenal prophecy", and "historical prefiguration". The Church Fathers,
too, especially Tertullian, Augustine, Irenaeus and Jerome, successfully defended the realism of typology against the excessive spiritual and purely
allegorical interpretations which had no basis in the *res ipsae* of scripture.

The antitype is sometimes called *veritas* and the type is often referred
to as *umbra* or *imago*. But this terminology, though apt to be confusing
at times, is strictly relative. Both the shadow and the image are abstract
only in relation to the truth, the fulfilled and perfected antitype. Shadow
and image are not abstract in themselves. Type and antitype are spiritual,

---

[1] Raymond E. Brown, S.S., "Hermeneutics", *The Jerome Biblical Commentary*, ed.
Raymond E. Brown *et al.* (Englewood Cliffs: Prentice-Hall, 1968), 619.

also, only with regard to the meaning they embody in the referential context of shadow and fulfillment. In themselves, and of themselves, they remain real things, not abstractions. Indeed, they would have no meaning at all as types if they were not scriptural realities, for the referential meaning of type and antitype rests essentially and necessarily upon the reality or concreteness of both poles of the reference. They are both *things*.

Moses, Joshua, Isaac, Adam are 'shadows' of Christ, but Moses, Joshua, Isaac and Adam are also real personages, and their relationship to their fulfillment in Christ, who is the Truth, does not diminish their own actual reality. They are real in themselves and real in their own historical context.

The Exodus was a type, a shadow of Baptism, but the Exodus was also a real event. Typology does not mean that the Old Testament types had no real meaning in themselves or for their contemporaries. It is foolish to maintain that they were understood and comprehensible only in the New Testament, and that the Old Testament typological events were intended for readers still to be born. The significance which they carried as types was a deeper significance in addition to their own reality. The Exodus had a meaning complete in itself, yet was seen as "more complete and meaningful" in the light of the New Testament antitype or fulfillment.

As Lampe points out when speaking of the vision of the Suffering Servant in Isaiah as a type of Christ:

This [typology] does not imply that the vision of the servant was not fully significant within its own limits, in relation to the Prophet's contemporary situation. We must not admit the absurd idea that the message of the prophets was meaningless or even incomplete for those to whom it was addressed, and that it was intended only for readers yet unborn. The Christian, however, will naturally look back on the Old Covenant with its fulfillment in Christ continually in mind, and he will be able to discern in the light of the fulfillment how the earlier stages in the working out of the divine purpose, each of which was significant for its own time, fall into place in an harmonious pattern and foreshadow the character of the final culmination.[2]

In the search for types, especially as these types are used in literature, one must be very careful not to strip the biblical account of its own intrinsic vitality. Dentan expresses this point very well when he says:

The men of the Bible were real men, engaged in actual conflicts in contemporary human situations, and not primarily concerned with fulfilling roles preordained by ancient types — or in tracing the fulfillment of such types.[3]

[2] G. W. H. Lampe, "The Reasonableness of Typology", *Essays on Typology*, 27.
[3] Dentan, "Typology — Its Use and Abuse", 216.

The tendency in examining types and antitypes is to overstress the anti-type, to emphasize the present fulfillment, and to look upon the Old Testament type as real only in relation to the present fulfillment. But to make the total essence and meaning of the type consist only in a pointing to and a foreshadowing of the fulfillment, destroys utterly the realism of the type in itself, and ultimately distorts the real nature of typology.

Typology, therefore, is much more than a metaphor or symbol. The symbol's whole existence is directed toward the thing which it signifies. Its essence is complete in its purely referential role; it is completely and essentially subordinated to the thing signified. But the type has genuine objective reality in and of itself, and as Brown indicates, it is only "mediately and secondarily that it signifies the antitype".[4]

The biblical metaphor or symbol does not possess this same realism. What basically differentiates the two is that typology "relates to an interpretation of history — indeed it is by nature a textual interpretation — while the symbol is a direct interpretation of life and originally no doubt, for the most part, of nature".[5] The relationship of type and antitype is a relationship of one *res* to another *res*, for which it prepares and which it foreshadows. Symbolism, on the other hand, establishes a relationship between the real and visible event or *res*, and a more real and invisible event.

Because of this basic concept of history biblical types can never be reduced completely to symbols. Their value and meaning depend essentially on their actuality as things related to each other. Typology, therefore, is primarily a historical method of scriptural exegesis. The Old Testament type has a significance for its contemporaries. But in addition to this significance, it is also a foreshadowing, a prefiguring of the New Testament antitype. But this added referential meaning does not destroy its own reality as a thing; the type and the antitype remain always literal and historically perceptible scriptural events, or *things*.

2. TYPOLOGY AND ALLEGORY

The failure to recognize and understand the reality or concreteness of both type and antitype in biblical exegesis has led to considerable mis-understanding and misinterpretation of biblical types and images. This

[4] Raymond E. Brown, S.S., *The Sensus Plenior in Sacred Scripture* (Baltimore: St. Mary's University Press, 1955), 10-11.
[5] Auerbach, "Figura", 57.

misunderstanding can reduce typology to a kind of biblical game where subjectivism runs wild in a "world of fantasy and intellectual will-o'-the-wisps"[6] and the biblical events provide fair game for the exercise of the reader's private ingenuity. Because of this neglect of the essential nature of both type and antitype as *things*, typology has also often been confused and unfairly condemned with the wild extravagances of the allegorical, symbolic, and mythical interpretations of scripture.[7]

Theodore of Mopsuestia, in his commentary on Galatians, strongly attacked those allegorists who, in his opinion, destroyed the obvious meaning of scripture and robbed it of its contents to manufacture stupid fables.[8] Richard Simon, whose *Critical History of the Old Testament* occasioned Dryden's *Religio Laici* and who has been considered the Father of modern biblical criticism,[9] recognized the danger of subjectivism in his own time:

It is not that I blame those who publish moral reflections on Scripture; but I do wish that they would not wander so far from the sense of the sacred authors. Because it is inevitable that under the pretext of moral reflections or of the spiritual sense of scripture, they fall into some nameless kind of jargon to which they give the name of spirituality.[10]

Even John Donne complained of:

... the underminings and batteries of hereticks and the curious refinings of the Allegoricall Fathers, which have made the Scriptures, which are strong toyles to catch and destroy the bore and bear which devast our Lord's vineyard, fine cobwebs to catch flies ...[11]

The essential distinction between typology and allegory was clearly made in the seventeenth-century by Johann Gerhard who wrote:

[6] Dentan, "Typology — Its Use and Abuse", 215. For a summary of Patristic typology and allegorical exegesis in brief form, see Charles Donohue, "Patristic Exegesis: Summation", *Critical Approaches to Medieval Literature*, ed. Dorothy Bethurum (New York: Columbia University Press, 1960).
[7] Richardson, "The Rise of Modern Biblical Scholarship ...", 336; Helen Gardner, *The Limits of Literary Criticism* (London: Oxford University Press, 1956), 52.
[8] Theodore of Mopsuestia, *In Epist, B. Pauli Commentarii, PG* 66.
[9] Louis I. Bredvold, *The Intellectual Milieu of John Dryden* (Ann Arbor: University of Michigan Press, 1959), 98 ff.
[10] "Ce n'est pas que je blâme ceux qui publient des réflexions morales sur l'Écriture; mais je souhaiterais qu'elles ne fussent pas si éloignées du sens des auteurs sacrés. Autrement il arrive que, sous prétexte de réflexions morales ou de sens spirituels, on tombe souvent dans je ne sais quel jargon, auquel on donne le nom de spiritualité." Cited in Joseph Coppens, *Les Harmonies des deux Testaments* (Tournai-Paris: Casterman, 1949), 80.
[11] *Essays In Divinity*, 40.

A type exists when some 'thing' in the Old Testament is shown to have pre-figured or foreshadowed something done or to be done in the New Testament. Allegory is when something from either the Old Testament or the New Testament is explained in some new way and is accommodated to some spiritual doctrine of the holy life. ... Typology consists in the comparison of facts. Allegory is concerned with the words themselves, from which it brings forth some useful, though recondite doctrine.[12]

There is a real difference between the use of allegory and typology even in the Fathers, and the crux of the distinction between the two forms of exegesis rests upon the essential reality of both terms in the typological interpretation, both the "signifying and the signified facts are real and concrete historical events. ... This is a very important point".[13] Both terms must be 'things'. Thus, Adam, Moses, or Joshua are types of Christ but they are also Adam, Moses, and Joshua. Their reality is not diminished by the typological reference to Christ. The historical and literal meaning of the biblical text, therefore, is essential and fundamental for typology, because the antitype builds upon the literal meaning of the type.

The allegorical interpretation of scripture takes little account of the historical reality. It rests upon an interpretation of scripture which is essentially unhistorical because it looks upon the Bible as a collection of oracles and riddles. The outward form, or letter, of the scriptural text conceals an inner, secret, mysterious meaning which must be discovered and analyzed by diligent search and study. The letter of the scriptures is only the outer shell which contains and, in a sense, conceals, the real meaning. Allegory becomes the search for these secondary and hidden meanings which underlie the primary and obvious literal meaning of the text and which often have little if any connection with the historical context of the narrative.

The exegete has to penetrate through the shell of history to the inner kernel of spiritual or moral truth. The whole range of the scriptures is one enormous field of symbolism in which the interpreter is free to wander at will, unrestricted by considerations of historical accuracy, the apparent intention of the biblical

---

[12] "Typus est cum factum aliquod Vet. Test. ostenditur praesignificasse seu adumbrasse aliquid gestum vel gerendum in Nov. Test. Allegoria est, cum aliquid ex Vet. vel Nov. Test. exponitur sensu novo atque accomodatur ad spiritualem doctrinam S. vitae. ... Typus consistit in factorum collatione. Allegoria occupatur non tam in factis, quam in ipsis concionibus, a quibus doctrinam utilem et reconditam depromit." The text is cited in E. Earle Ellis, *Paul's Use of the Old Testament*, 127 and note. Ellis translates "concionibus" as 'assembly' and therefore the distinction between allegory and type makes little sense.

[13] Auerbach, *Typological Symbolism in Medieval Literature*, 6. See also "Figura", 84.

authors, or the superficial diversity of their outlook. He can gather his symbolism whence he pleases and combine it into any pattern which he may happen to fancy.[14]

Markus points out the obvious and inevitable conclusion: "Once the exegete's hold on the literal sense is loosened and the straightforward narrative or historical sense is allowed to slip into the background, appeal can only be made to something outside the text for a criterion of what it means."[15] This is precisely what allegory does, for it is based not upon the literal, historical meaning of the text but upon some moral or theological system which is completely extrinsic to the biblical texts, and which is merely illustrated by the use of images drawn from the text. Danielou can therefore conclude with good reason that: "Allegory is not a sense of scripture at all; it is the presentation of philosophy and Christian morality under biblical images."[16] The danger in allegorical exegesis:

... lies less in its sheer artificiality than in its encouragement to the reader to ignore history, to treat the bible unhistorically, and, in defiance of the solid achievements of the critical approach, to regard the whole of Scripture as a bundle of oracles from which any and every expositor can quarry pieces at random to fashion into a mosaic of his own design. ... I have elsewhere (*Theology*, June, 1953) alluded to 'that dangerous territory between typology and allegory where parallels begin to be forced into the text by artificial playing with words, instead of being naturally suggested by it,' and I have in the same place complained of the prevalence of jugglery with words and etymologies.[17]

This type of allegorical interpretation of scripture has been identified most often with Philo and the Alexandrian school of biblical exegesis. Philo's technique of allegory presumed a hidden meaning almost everywhere in the biblical text which was to be 'discovered' by the trained exegete. But the danger is that we are nowhere given any objective evidence for the existence of this hidden and allegorical meaning. It remains purely subjective because there is no external norm, no rule of thumb, to aid in evaluating this hidden meaning. The critic is indeed free to wander at will in the forests of scripture, taking and using what he

[14] Lampe, "The Reasonableness of Typology", 31.
[15] R. A. Markus, "Presuppositions of the Typological Approach to Scripture", *The Communication of the Gospel in New Testament Times*, ed. Austin Farrar et al. (London: SPCK, 1961), 77.
[16] J. Danielou, *From Shadows to Reality*, 61.
[17] Lampe, "The Reasonableness of Typology", 31, 36. See also pp. 30-36 for a fuller summary of the differences between Allegory and Typology. For a discussion of the critical positions on the relationship of Typology and Allegory, see James Barr, *Old and New in Interpretation* (London: SCM Press, Ltd., 1966), 103-148.

will, ignoring and overlooking as he pleases. The result is inevitably a highly subjective interpretation of scripture.

A good example of this sort of allegorizing is Origen's account of the Parable of the Good Samaritan in Luke, with its detailed allegorical interpretation for each of the elements in the parable.

The man means Adam with the life he originally led and with the fall caused by disobedience. Jerusalem means Paradise, or the Jerusalem on high. Jericho is the world, the robbers are the opposing powers, whether devils or false teachers, who profess to come in the name of Christ. The wounds are disobedience and sins. Man is stripped of his clothing, that is, he loses incorruptibility and immortality, he is despoiled of every virtue. He is left half dead because death has seized a half of our human nature. The priest is the law. The Levite represents the prophets. The Samaritan is Christ who took on human flesh through Mary. The beast of burden is the body of Christ. The wine is the word of teaching and correction, the oil is the word of philanthropy, compassion or encouragement. The Inn is the Church. The innkeeper is the college of the apostles and their successors, bishops and teachers of the Church, or else the angels who are set over the church. The two pennies are the two testaments, the Old and the New, or love of God and one's neighbor, or knowledge of the Father and the Son. The return from Samaria is the second coming of Christ.[18]

Other examples of allegory which abound in the Fathers make the subjective nature of this method of exegesis quite clear. In Genesis, for example, God created Adam, that is the spiritual soul, and then gave him a companion, Eve, who represents sensation and the passions. The four rivers of Paradise, or the four beasts of Ezechiel, represent the four evangelists.[19] The sons of Noah are three in number and therefore they stand for those who believe in the Trinity. Similarly, the three days before the creation of light in Genesis also represent the Trinity.[20] The seven women in Isaiah who siezed one man are the seven gifts of the Holy Spirit. Because this type of allegory does not have any objective rules, it is virtually impossible, in Musurillo's phrasing which has been discussed above, to derive the precise meaning of a text, its connotation and denotation, or to say that X is the meaning and Y is not.[21]

It is true that the dividing line between allegory and typology is some-

---

[18] *Hom. 34 in Lucam*, *PG* 13:1336-7. See similar allegorical interpretations in Augustine, *Enarr.* in Ps. 126: 15, *PL* 37:1666-7; Ambrose, *Expositiones in Evangelium Secundum Lucam*, 7:71ff., *PL* 15:1805-7, and Severus of Antioch, *Homily* 89, *Patrologia Orientalis*, 23:105-114.

[19] Jerome, *Comm. in Evangelium Matthei*, *PL* 26:19; Pseudo-Jerome, *In Evangelium Sec. Mattheum*, *PL* 30:551a: Smaragdus, *Collectiones in Epistolas et Evangelia*, *PL* 102:333b.

[20] Theophilus of Antioch, *Ad Autolycum* 2:15, *PG* 6:1077.

[21] Musurillo, "Shadow and Reality: Thoughts on the Problem of Typology", 458.

times difficult to discern, and at times even more difficult to define accurately. Danielou calls Book XII of Augustine's *Contra Faustum* a treatise on typology,[22] but it could just as well be called a treatise on allegory. Paul's use of the Melchisedech image in the Epistle to the Hebrews has often been cited as an example of typology. But as Lampe points out so well: "There is no clear correspondence between the type and the fulfillment, and no genuine historical recapitulation of a single pattern of the divine activity."[23] It is based only on a supposed lack of ancestry. Yet a case could just as easily be made for Melchisedech as a genuine type of Christ in the context of the whole Epistle.

Critics also differ in calling the Hagar imagery in Galatians 4 either allegory or strict typology.[24] But whether allegory or type, it is clear that Paul's use of Hagar and Sarah is definitely historically oriented, and it is the historical pattern of the story of Sarah and Hagar which is used as a pattern or type of God's dealings with the Old and the New Israel. Paul's interpretation is firmly anchored to history and is thus preserved from extravagance. This is entirely different from Philo's use of the same story where the historical pattern plays no part at all.[25] Philo's interpretation is pure allegory, in which the names of Sarah and Hagar are interpreted allegorically and used to uncover the underlying senses of the narrative. Paul's use of the story is not exactly the same. Is Paul's account, therefore, to be called allegory or typology? It is hard to draw the line accurately between the two.

The same difficulty arises, for example, from Theodoret's remarks on the events of Exodus: "The Red Sea is a type of the baptismal font; the cloud, of the Holy Spirit; Moses, of the Saviour Christ; his rod, of the cross; Pharoah, of the devil; the Egyptians, of the demons; manna, of the Eucharistic food; and the water which sprang from the rock, of the saving blood of Christ."[26] Is this type or allegory? Woollcombe says: "This is virtually allegorism got up in typological dress."[27] But what is *virtual* allegory?

Although in some cases it is difficult to distinguish allegory and type,

[22] J. Danielou, "Traversée de la Mer Rouge et Baptisme aux premiers siècles", *Recherches de Science Religieuse*, XXXIII (1946), 420.
[23] Lampe, "The Reasonableness of Typology", 34.
[24] "Even in this passage ... one finds an interpretation more in accord with Pauline typology than with Alexandrian allegory." — Ellis, *Paul's Use of the Old Testament*, 53, 130.
[25] Philo, *De Congressu Eruditionis Gratiae*, 23, *Opera Omnia*, Tomus III (Lipsiae: Sumptibus Holtze, 1892).
[26] Theodoret, *Quaestiones in Exodum*, 27, *PG* 80:257.
[27] Woollcombe, "The Biblical Origins and Patristic Development of Typology", 60.

it should be abundantly clear that typology is something very different from subjective and "uncontrolled allegorizing on Old Testament ... texts". For allegory:

... there is no criterion given in the text itself of what is allowable and what is arbitrary importation. The case is different with spiritual exegesis of the Old Testament; although it cannot itself provide the criterion of its 'spiritual' (or 'typological' — the terminology does not matter) senses, these criteria can be discovered in the New Testament.[28]

The prudent and intelligent application of the criteria here suggested — the realism of the 'thing', the recapitulative nature of typology which depends upon a metaphysical correspondence and the notion of fulfillment in type and antitype, and the essential notion of divine resonance and Christic correspondence in the typological structure — should do much to dissipate the confusion and subjectivism in the determination of true types, especially when distinguished from allegory.

3. THE METAPHYSICAL CORRESPONDENCE OF TYPE AND ANTITYPE

The distinction between typology and allegory is based primarily on the reality of both terms of the relationship. But allegory can also be confused with genuine and legitimate typological interpretation because, although both terms of the relationship are 'things', the link or correspondence between them depends upon an arbitrary and extrinsic interpretation. In strict typology there must be an objective and essential correspondence existing between the poles of the relationship. Allegory undermines not only the reality of both type and antitype as 'thing', but it also tends to destroy the relationship, the typological link, between the two terms as well, and make it an artificial and purely subjective relationship.[29]

Typology has been defined as the relationship between Old Testament and New Testament events, persons and things. But this relationship must be a metaphysical correspondence which does not depend upon arbitrary or accidental details, but is based upon some notable and essential quality in the notions of both type and antitype. The metaphysical relationship, as well as both terms of the typological correspondence, must be real and intelligible. It must make a reasonable appeal to the intellect, rather than an arbitrary appeal to the imagination.[30] Theodore

---

[28] Markus, "Presuppositions of the Typological Approach to Scripture", 80.
[29] G. W. H. Lampe, "The Reasonableness of Typology", 33-34.
[30] Woollcombe, "Le Sens de 'type' chez les Pères", p. 86. See also A. M. Dubarle, "Le sens spirituel de l'Écriture", Revue SR, XXXI (1947), 43.

of Mopsuestia emphasizes this metaphysical correspondence between the type and the antitype: "It is surely obvious that every type has some resemblance to that which it is said to typify." But Theodore insists that the correspondence must be an "organic relationship" (μίμησις); it cannot depend upon merely superficial or accidental details. The correspondence belongs to the essence of both type and antitype.[31]

Typology is essentially historically oriented, not only with regard to the actual phenomenal reality of both type and antitype, but also with regard to the link that is established between the two terms in a historical context. Typology demands what Burlin calls "a historical continuum" between its two terms.[32] Allegory, on the other hand, makes no attempt to trace a genuine relationship of similar structure between the two terms. The correspondence between them, in the allegorical interpretation, depends upon arbitrary and accidental details which are taken almost at random to represent facts or ideas of an entirely different nature. In allegory, the added referential meaning is actually foreign to the ideas conveyed by the literal meaning of the words and events in the Old Testament.[33]

This metaphysical correspondence is clear in the classic examples of typology in Paul and in the Fathers. There is no doubt, for example, of the essential relationship between Adam and Christ. It is not just accidental details which establish Christ as a Second Adam in the history of salvation, or the Exodus and the Pasch as a type of the Christian's salvation in the New Testament.[34] The case is entirely different with the so-called 'type' of Rahab which was so frequently used by the Fathers. The scarlet ribbon suspended by the courtesan Rahab from the wall of Jericho in the second chapter of the Book of Joshua is not genuinely typological since it fails to establish a meaningful and metaphysically significant link between type and antitype. As Dom Charlier points out:

The scarlet ribbon has no other connection with the blood of Christ than its color and a functional similarity which is completely external: it saved Rahab, and the blood of Christ saves the Christian. But is this sufficient for affirming that the Holy Spirit has hidden a prefiguration of one under the other? No literal bond unites the red ribbon and the redeeming blood. One did not take rise from the other; faith in the second did not spring from the contemplation of the first. It is completely different, for example, with the Paschal Lamb,

[31] *Commentarius in Michaeam Prophetam*, 4:1, *PG* 66:364d. See also *Commentarius in Jonam Prophetam*, *PG* 66:320-321.
[32] Robert B. Burlin, *The Old English Advent: A Typological Commentary* (New Haven: Yale University Press, 1968), IX, 6.
[33] Mickelson, *Interpreting the Bible*, 261.
[34] Romans 5:14; I Corinthians 10:6, 11.

or with the blood which Moses sprinkled on the people in order to consecrate the Alliance, at the foot of Sinai; these rites efficaciously give start, in the religious conscience of Israel, to an opening movement subject to the revelation of the sense of the Passion, on the Day of the New Alliance, and they efficaciously prepared, in the history of the people of God, the objective germination of the event.[35]

W. J. Phythian-Adams uses the term 'homology' to describe this metaphysical correspondence between type and antitype in typology. By homology he means "... that there is between two things not a mere resemblance but a real and vital — in this case an economic — correspondence". Talking of the New Creation which is one nature with the Old, he says: "To use a scientific term, there is not merely an analogy, but a real homology, an intimate creaturely relationship between them. ... When we observe closely the system of created nature we find underlying it a principle of co-ordination and integration which builds it up through an ascending series of stages into an ordered structure of 'wholes'."[36] Phythian-Adams bases his principle of homology on Smuts' definition of a 'whole' (Greek: ὅλος) as a "specific structural synthesis of parts with inner activities of its own which cooperate and function in harmony ... towards a definite inherent end or purpose", and in borrowing this scientific term, Phythian-Adams says that this principle of homology "is for the Christian nothing else than the manifestation of the Creative Spirit".[37]

Yet as R. A. Markus indicates,[38] there is a basic danger in this concept of homology. The emphasis on the 'overall similarity' of the two Testaments tends to multiply possibilities of finding fanciful as well as genuine types. Within the framework of this sort of homology, subjective allegorizing finds fertile soil and, at its worst, a general theory of homology tends to overlook the basic similarity between type and antitype.

[35] Dom Celestin Charlier, "Méthode historique et lecture spirituelle des Écritures", *Bible et Vie Chretienne*, No. 18 (June-August, 1957). The translation is by John F. McCall in William F. Lynch, *Christ and Apollo*, 265-266. Lampe, 34 says: "... there is no real type here". For additional patristic uses of Rahab, see the references in H. E. W. Turner, *The Pattern of Christian Truth* (London: A. R. Mowbray and Company, Ltd., 1954), 281-283.

[36] W. J. Phythian-Adams, *The Way of At-One-Ment* (London: Oxford University Press, 1944), 11 and *The People and the Presence* (London: Oxford University Press, 1942), 254-255.

[37] J. C. Smuts, *Holism and Evolution* (New York: The Macmillan Company, 1929), 107, cited in Phythian-Adams, *The People and the Presence*, 255. For other references to Phythian-Adams' Principle of Homology, see A. G. Hebert, *The Authority of the Old Testament*, 218-222 and E. Earle Ellis, *Paul's Use of the Old Testament*, 128.

[38] R. A. Markus, "Presuppositions ...", 80.

Far simpler, and less likely to confuse, is Woollcombe's interpretation of a passage from Chrysostom, where Isaac carrying the wood for his sacrifice is compared with Christ carrying his cross. Chrysostom says: "And now they laid the cross upon him as a malefactor. For even the wood they abominated and endured not even to touch it. This was also the case in the type; for Isaac bore the wood. But then the matter (πρᾶγμα) stopped, at the will of his father, for it was the type (τύπος); while here it proceeded to action, for it was the reality (ἀλήθεια)." Woollcombe points out that the significant words in the passage are τύπος (the type), αλήθεια (the antitype), and πρᾶγμα (the 'matter', which is the purpose of God).[39]

At the sacrifice of Isaac it (πρᾶγμα) "stood still" in the type, i.e. it remained concealed. But at the sacrifice of Christ it "came out" and was made plain. The πρᾶγμα was common to both type and antitype, but it was present in each in a different degree of revelation. In Chrysostom's typology, therefore, the two parts of the type-pair were revelations differing in magnitude, of a single πρᾶγμα in the divine purpose; hence the types had a force which only differed in magnitude from the force of their antitypes, and were no less real and divinely willed.[40] The πρᾶγμα, the 'matter' inherent in both type and antitype as a revelation of the divine purpose, is the metaphysical basis for the relationship of the two terms in a typological context. This basis is not accidental or arbitrary. It is real and essential to both the type and the antitype. It also unites them in a metaphysical correspondence which is much more than mere accident. The πρᾶγμα is the discoverable divine will in both terms, the essential metaphysical similarity or correspondence, which links both type and antitype together in a fundamental relationship.

4. FULFILLMENT AND RECAPITULATION

In the Epistles of Paul and the exegesis of the Fathers, the relationship of the two Testaments was always that of imperfect to perfect. The Old Testament prefigured the New; the New Testament was an advance and a fulfillment of the Old. There was no antithesis, no contradiction between the two Testaments, but rather a very basic evolutionary unity. The Old Testament had a historical function to fulfill, complete in itself, but its

---

[39] *Homilia LXXXV in Joannem, PG* 59:459.
[40] K. J. Woollcombe, "The Biblical Origins and Patristic Development of Typology", 73.

function was also to prepare for the New. This principle is essential to the notion of typology, which is but one manifestation of the relationship of the Old and the New Testament in God's providential history of salvation. Both the type and the antitype, as has been seen, were historical realities. They were both actual and phenomenal events. But, as Auerbach maintains, the antitype or the fulfillment in the New Testament possessed the character of historical reality in greater and more intense measure, for it is, "compared with the figure, *forma perfectior*".[41] Bishop Gaudentius of Brescia described the Figure, the type in the Old Testament, as *imitatio veritatis* rather than as *veritas ipsa*.[42] The same idea appears in I Peter 1:19, where the author compares the type and the antitype as candle and star. The words of the prophets will "go on shining like a candle in a dark room, until the dawn breaks and the day-star rises in your hearts". Origen uses a very similar image when he speaks of the shadow:

The apostle says that the Law is the shadow of good things to come. Thus those who were under the Law were under its shadow. But we are no longer under the Law, but under Divine Grace. Although we are no longer under the shadow of the Law, we are, however, under a better shadow. Truly we live in the shadow of Christ among nations.[43]

In genuine typology, the antitype must 'fulfill' the type. The technical term used by the Fathers is "*figuram implere*".

St. Augustine emphasises this notion of fulfillment, of *forma perfectior*, in the New Testament antitypes. Time and time again he reiterates the dictum that the New Testament is latent in the Old, the Old Testament is patent in the New.[44] In *De Spiritu et Littera* he speaks of the observances of the Law "... which Christians now cast aside as mere shadows of the age to come, possessing as they do that which was promised in a figure by these shadows".[45]

---

[41]   Erich Auerbach, *Mimesis*, p. 197. Similarly, Bonsirven says: "Le type est déficient, inferieur ... le prototype ... il est exemplaire suprême dont ses analogues ne presentent que des participations, des approximations de plus en plus dégradées." J. Bonsirven, "Saint Paul et l'Ancien Testament", *Nouvelle Revue Théologique*, LXV (1938), 134.
[42]   "Figura etenim non est veritas sed imitatio veritatis ..." — *De Exodi Lectione*, II, *PL* 20:855.
[43]   *Com. Cant.* III, *PG* 13:153. See also *Hom. Los.*, 8:4.
[44]   "Signum veteris testamenti ciicumcisio in latenti carne; signum novi testamenti crux in libera fronte. Ibi enim occultatio est; hic revelatio; illud est sub velamine, hoc in facie." — *Sermo* 95:6, *PL* 38:876. For other examples: *Quaest. in Hept.*, II, 73, 103, *PL* 34:623, 633, and *De Doct. Christ.*, III, 37, *PL* 34:88.
[45]   "... quas tamquam umbras futuri saeculi nunc respuunt Christiani, id tenentes quod per illas umbras figurate promittebatur." — 14:23, *PL* 44.

Melito's image of the sculptor's model which has been discussed above also brings out very clearly the relationship of model to statue, figure to fulfillment, in the typological relationship. Like Melito, both Origen and Chrysostom said that the pattern or model was worthless when it had fulfilled its purpose and was to be discarded.[46] The *forma inferior* had outlived its usefulness in the presence of the *forma perfectior*. The type was fulfilled and perfected in the antitype.

The Law then, and everything in the Law, being inspired, as the Apostle says, until the time of amendment, is like those people whose job it is to make statues and cast them in metal. Before they tackle the statue itself, the one they are going to cast in bronze, silver, or in gold, they first make a clay model to show what they are aiming at. The model is a necessity but only until the real statue is finished. The model is made for the sake of the statue, and when the statue is ready, the sculptor has no further use for the model. Well, it is rather like that with the Law and the Prophets. The things written in the Law and the Prophets were meant as types or figures of things to come. But now the artist himself has come, the Author of it all, and he has cast the Law aside, because it contained only the shadows of the good things to come (Hebrews 10:1) whereas He brought the things themselves.[47]

Delporte calls the type an anticipated image of a future reality, a Vorbild. But it is not strictly a portrait; it is rather, as Hebrews affirms, a silhouette of the future reality.[48]

It is extremely important to note, however, that the antitype is a fulfillment, not a destruction of the type. It is only in relation to the antitype that the type is *forma inferior*. The model has a value and a beauty all its own. It is inferior only in relation to the completed statue. The type is composed, in Tresmontant's interpretation:

... of an empirical aspect and a metaphysical one, of a contingent actuality, recorded and past, and of a substantial sign which, far from being obsolete, appears to us more and more significant and true as history unfolds.[49]

[46] Origen, *Hom. 10:2 in Phil.*
[47] Origen, *Hom. 10:1 in Lev.*, PG 12:525. See pp. 20-21.
[48] "Je veux bien que le type soite l'image anticipée d'une realité future, 'ein Vorbild,' disent les Allemands; mais ce n'est pas un portrait, c'est une 'silhouette' — le mot est de l'Épître des Hébreux (Heb. 10:1, 8:5)." — Lucien Delporte, "Les principes de la Typologie Biblique ...", 308.
[49] Claude Tresmontant, *A Study of Hebrew Thought*, trans. Michael Francis Gibson (New York: Desclee Company, 1960), 73. Basil expresses the same idea in more figurative language: "Come, let us walk not in the light of the Prophets or the Law, but in the light of the Lord. Lamps have their place, but only before sunrise; stars have their beauty, but only in the night. If we think a man is ridiculous to have a lighted lamp in full daylight, how much more ridiculous when the Gospel has been proclaimed, to linger in the shadow of the law." — PG 30:445c.

Origen brings out this point in a simile which is perhaps more clear than the model image:

Lamps are useful as long as people are in the dark; they cease to be a help when the sun rises. The glory on the face of Moses is of use to us, and so, it seems to me, is the glory on the prophets' faces; it is beautiful to look at and it helps us see how glorious Christ is. We needed to see their glory before we could see his. But their glory paled before the greater glory of Christ. In the same way there has to be a partial knowledge first and later, when perfect knowledge is acquired, it will be discarded. ... But the majority of people do not see the beauty of the many pearls in the law and the gnosis (partial though it is) of the prophetical books. They imagine that although they have not thoroughly plumbed and fathomed the depths of these works, they will yet be able to find the one pearl of great cost and contemplate the supremely excellent gnosis, which is the knowledge of Christ. Yet this form of gnosis is so superior to the others that in comparison with it they seem like stercora, though they are not stercora by nature. ... And anyone who wants to become learned in the words of truth must first be taught the rudiments and gradually master them; he must hold them, too, in high esteem. He will not, of course, remain all the time, at this elementary level; he will be like a man who thought highly of the rudiments at first and now that he has advanced beyond them to perfection, is still grateful to them for their introductory work and their former services. In the same way, when the things that are written in the Law and prophets are fully understood, they become the rudiments on which perfect understanding of the Gospels and all spiritual knowledge of Christ's words and deeds are based.[50]

The real value of the Law is brought out clearly in this passage. The Law has a glory all its own, a *gnosis* which represents a stage through which man must pass. It is only when a greater glory, a superior *gnosis* appears, that the types of the Old Testament are seen as inferior, more rudimentary reflections of a higher, more perfect form.[51] It is, as Origen says elsewhere, that Isaac, the type of Christ, is small in the Law, a mere child. He grows in the prophets, but when he becomes man, the veil is completely taken away.[52]

It may legitimately be said, then, that the typological relationship of the antitype as the *forma perfectior* of the type, is recapitulative. The antitype reiterates or repeats the original type, but it also consummates and sums up, perfects and completes the original.

... the recapitulative nature of the saving acts of God in Christ ... is at the heart of typology. Irenaeus, having stated that Christ summed up the entire human race with Adam himself, was perfectly justified in concluding: "Therefore,

[50] *Comm. Matt.*, 10:9-10, *PG* 13:856-876.
[51] Jean Danielou, *Origen*, 146.
[52] "Parvus est Isaac in lege, sed processu temporis fit magnus." — *Hom.* 12:5 in *Gen.*, *PG* 12:228.

Adam was said by Paul to be τύπος τοῦ μέλλοντος because the Word, who made all things, had formed beforehand for himself the Economy of mankind which would center in the Son of God; God predestinating the natural man to be saved by the spiritual man" (*Adv. Haer.*, IV, 22,2).[53]

It is true that the notion of recapitulation, in theological terminology, is more strictly limited to the nature of Christ's redemptive actions, and bears reference only to the Christ-Adam type. This is clear in Molwitz's definition: "Recapitulation is the repetition of Adam, through similarities and contrasts, made perfect by Christ with the intention that he might bring all things into subjection to himself."[54] But it is a legitimate extension to apply the notion of recapitulation to typology in general, and to say with some foundation that every antitype is recapitulative of its Old Testament type. For recapitulation includes the notion of historical similitude as well as the notion of the fulfillment, the *forma perfectior* that has already been discussed. The notion of recapitulation in the exegesis of Paul and of Irenaeus sums up, therefore, in one convenient term two of the essential elements of type — the metaphysical correspondence and the idea of fulfillment. Christ repeats Adam; there is a metaphysical relationship between the two. But Christ also perfects Adam; he is a more perfect Adam, the true fulfillment of Adam. There is a similarity between the two, but also a difference, an improvement. In typological terms, Adam 'points to' Christ. There is a basic relationship between them. But Christ is also a more perfect Adam, like him in many ways, but also endowed with qualities quite foreign to the Adam of Genesis. Christ is a 'heightened' Adam, or to use Goppelt's term, there is a definite *Steigerung* in Christ which is not present in Adam.[55] These two elements — the type pointing to the antitype, and the antitype summing up the type, the heightened pattern and the *forma perfectior* of the typological relationship — form the basis of the antitype as recapitulative of the type.

---

[53] Woollcombe, "The Biblical Origins and Patristic Development of Typology", 49. For Irenaeus's views on recapitulation, see John Lawson, *The Biblical Theology of Saint Irenaeus* (London: Epworth Press, 1948), 140ff.

[54] "Recapitulatio est iteratio Adami (per idem ac contrarium) a Christo eo consilio, perfecta, ut omnia sibi subjiceret." — Gustav Molwitz, *De 'Ανακεφαλαισεως in Irenaei Theologia Potestate*, cited in Lawson, *The Biblical Theology of Saint Irenaeus*, 140.

[55] Dentan, "Typology — Its Use and Abuse", 214. For a lengthier interpretation of other theological views on recapitulation, cf. Lawson, 140-144.

5. DIVINE RELEVANCE AND CHRISTIC CORRESPONDENCE

The final element of genuine typological structure is what might be called the Relevance of the Divine. In Gribement's words,"... typology is not an attribute of brute things taken in themselves, entirely abstracted from the faith of Israel and the prophetic charism".[56] Goppelt makes the same point: "Typology shows not only the character of the New in relation to the Old, but also that it rests directly and solely on the foundation of Salvation History."[57] The whole notion of typology, therefore, must be fitted into the context of the divine providence of God in governing and controlling history. In this conception, the relationship between type and antitype is not necessarily a chronological or causal development, but rather a "oneness within the divine plan, of which all occurrences are parts and reflections. Their direct earthly connection is of secondary importance, and often their interpretation can altogether dispense with any knowledge of it."[58] Both type and antitype must have some basic quality or similitude in common, as has been seen. But this common element should also exhibit God's purpose in the historical context of both type and antitype. Without this divine relevance in the historical context, there really cannot be any typology.

When Paul speaks of the events of the Exodus happening τυπικῶς and written "for our admonition",[59] there can be no doubt that in Paul's mind the "divine intent is of the essence" in these events, "both in their occurrence and in their inscripturation". The rationale of New Testament exegesis is not only "the continuity of God's purpose throughout His covenant, but also His Lordship in moulding and using history to reveal and illumine His purpose. God writes His parallels in the sands of Time."[60]

[56] "... la typologie n'est pas un attribut des choses brutes en elles-mêmes, abstraction faite de la foi d'Israel et du charisme prophétique". Cited R. E. Brown, *The Sensus Plenior in Sacred Scripture* (Baltimore: St. Mary's University Press, 1955), 14. Also in similar fashion: Typology ... "c'est l'ensemble de significations relatives a l'histoire du salut chrétien, sous sa double phase; temporelle ou messianique, éternelle ou eschatologique, qui se dégagent des personnes et des gestes de l'histoire biblique, surtout de l'Ancien Testament, en tant qu'elles ont été façonnées, groupées et dirigées par La Providence pour préfigurer d'avance l'avenir." — Joseph Coppens, *Les Harmonies des Deux Testaments*, 82-83.

[57] "Die Typologie zeigt nicht nur das Wesen des Neuen gegenuber dem Alten, sondern such dass es gerade und nur auf diesem heilsgeschichtlichen Grunde steht." — Leonhard Goppelt, *Typos: Die Typologische Deutung des Alten Testaments im Neuen* (Gutersloh: C. Bertelsmann, 1939), 183.

[58] Auerbach, *Mimesis*, 490.

[59] I Corinthians 10:11; cf. also Romans 5:14 and I Peter 3:21.

[60] Ellis, *Paul's Use of the Old Testament*, 127-128.

To arrive at a deeper understanding of typology, the reader must come to a full awareness of one of the most dominant themes of the Bible. This is that in both the Old and the New Testaments, God is not an abstraction. He is always "our God", a God who is very real and vitally concerned in the lives of historical men. He is not an aloof Olympian deity uninterested in the ways of men. In every sense of the word, He is a God who acts and reveals himself to mankind through the progressive and deeper revelation of his salvific plan for mankind. He is a God who remembers what He has said and who builds upon what he has said and done before. "He has protected his servant Israel, keeping his merciful design in remembrance, according to the promise which he made to our forefathers, Abraham and his posterity for evermore."[61]

The Bible, which is God's word, is therefore a unique book. It, truly,

... is not a book like the others. Inspired by the Holy Spirit, its dimensions have nothing in common with the books of men. The Word of God is truly expressed not only in words and in ideas; it also manifests itself to us, without exhausting itself even there, in the events of a history which is holy. When the Lord wished to speak to men, he began by instituting a People; and, by a slow teaching process, he led this people from Moses to Jesus. The Bible is nothing else than a living account of the impact of Israel in the Old and in the New Covenant. ... The ledger of the people of God, the Bible is at the same time for each one of us the Word of God, the Revelation of God, the source of life. In other words, the words and images of Scripture go far beyond themselves. They have an infinite resonance. They are bearers of a message of divine life.[62]

This concept of the divine resonance is a fundamental notion in the fuller understanding of typology. The Old Testament type is not only a historical reality with a metaphysical correspondence to the New Testament antitype. The New Testament antitype is not only a fulfillment, a *forma perfectior*, of the type. Both terms, and in fact, the relationship itself, are possessed of a resonance which is divine. They literally echo with God. God's provident hand touches the world and history and

[61] Luke 1:54-55.
[62] "La Bible n'est pas un livre comme les autres. Inspiré par l'Esprit-Saint, ses dimensions sont sans commune mesure avec les ouvrages des homnes. La Parole de Dieu ne s'exprime pas seulement, en effet, dans des mots et des idées; elle se manifeste aussi à nous, sans s'y épuiser, dans les événements d'une histoire qui est sainte. Lorsque le Seigneur a voulu parler aux hommes, il a commencé par constituer un peuple; et, par une lente pédagogie, il a mené ce peuple de Moise à Jésus. La Bible n'est pas autre chose qu'une receuil vivant des témoignages sur l'événement de l'ancienne et de la nouvelle alliance ... Livre de raison du peuple de Dieu, La Bible est en même temps pour chacun de nous la Parole de Dieu, la Révélation de Dieu, source de vie. C'est dire que les mots et les images de l'Écriture vont plus loin qu'eux-mêmes. Ils ont résonance infinie. Ils sont porteurs d'un message de vie divine." — René Beaupère, O.P., "La Bible, source de l'imaginaire chrétien", *La Vie Spirituelle*, No. 472 (Mai, 1961), 497-498.

time, and at each touch, divine echoes are set up which reverberate and reinforce one another across the barriers of historical time. As will be seen in greater detail in the following chapter, this divine resonance is actually the result of the impact of Eternity upon historical time, of the meeting of the Infinite and the finite at a given moment in the historical evolution of God's salvific will.

The divine resonance of the typological structure is truly infinite. It is effectual not only in the past, in the Old Testament, and in the present in the New Testament, but it also extends into the future, reaching out to the ἔσχατον at the end of time. God is revealed in time — in the past in the Old Testament types, and in the present in the New Testament anti-types. But time will have an end, and God will reveal Himself a third time, in a second and greater antitype, at the end of time, the ἔσχατον. This is the foundation for the triple typological structure which is seen in many of the early Fathers and especially in Augustine. The Old Testament figure is a type of the New Testament fulfillment which it foreshadows. But both these terms are at the same time prefigurations and foreshadowings of similar events at the end of time. Thus, just as the Old Testament is a shadow of the New, the New Testament is in turn a shadow of the Kingdom to come at the end of world. As Junilius writes: "The intention of the Old Testament is to point to the New by figures and prophesies; that of the New is to kindle the minds of men to eternal beatitude."[63]

The typological element of fulfillment in the *forma perfectior* is thus accomplished in three successive stages, rather than just two. The his-torical Christ of the New Testament is a greater Adam, but the heavenly Christ ruling the Kingdom of men at the end of time will be an even greater Adam. For this reason, Ambrose can say: "The Shadow is in the Law; The Image in the Gospel; and the Truth will be in Heaven."[64] But this one element of fulfillment is not enough to characterize the threefold relationship as truly typological. If the relationship is to be considered truly typological, all three terms must be historical realities, even though the third exists only in a historical future, and the metaphysical corre-

---

[63] "Veteris (Testamenti) intentio est Novum figuris denuntiationibusque monstrare; Novi autem ad Aeternae beatitudinis gloriam humanas mentes accendere." — Junilius, *Instituta Regularia Diversae Legis*, ch. 10, *PL* 68:20. See also Origen, *In Canticum Canticorum*, 3, *PG* 13:153.

[64] "Umbra in lege. Imago vero in Evangelio. Veritas in Coelestibus.", Ambrose, *Enarratio in Ps.* 38:25, *PL* 14:1101. These three words: *Umbra, imago, Veritas*, are the words used most commonly by the Fathers to designate the threefold development of the type. See the discussion of this anagogical typology in the Appendix.

spondence based upon the essential homology or matter must exist in all three terms.

With this threefold structure of typology as a basis, then, Origen can speak of three Passovers — the historical Passover in the Old Testament, the Passover of the Last Supper, and the heavenly Passover at the end of time — and of three Peoples — the Old Israel, the Church, and the Kingdom of Heaven.[65] It is Augustine, however, who gives perhaps the clearest expression to this threefold typological development:

For we are all aware that the Old Testament contains promises of temporal things and that is why it is called the Old Testament; and that the promise of eternal life and the kingdom of heaven belongs to the New Testament; but that in these temporal figures there was a promise of future things which were to be fulfilled in us on whom the ends of the world are come, is no fantasy of mine, but the interpretation of the Apostles, as Paul says speaking of these matters ...[66]

It must be admitted, however, that many critics do not consider the fulfillment at the end of time a true typological element. They prefer to restrict typology to Old and New Testament parallels, and eliminate the third stage of development in the heavenly kingdom. It certainly is difficult, if not impossible, to verify the elements of true typology in the eschatological fulfillment in any but an analogical sense. It is impossible, for example, to verify the reality of the third element, and therefore the metaphysical correspondence and the notion of fulfillment are difficult to determine. The eschatological antitype can hardly be said to be phenomenal or actual. The present 'unreality' of this third element also opens the door once again to every variety of subjective allegory. Therefore it is perhaps best to consider typology as existing only in two terms — the Old Testament type and the New Testament antitype.

This fourth element of typology, the divine relevance of God in history, can be summarized by affirming that all genuine typology must be Christological. There must be a Christic correspondence between the typological terms, but it is extremely important to understand exactly what is meant when this terminology is used. Typology is

---

[65] Origen, *Comm. in Mt.*, 17:9, *PG* 13:1504-1505; *Comm. in Jn.* X, 16:8, *PG* 14:346ff.; *Homilia I in Ps.* 38, *PG* 12:1402-1403.

[66] "Temporalium quidem rerum promissiones Testamento Veteri contineri; et ideo Vetus Testamentum appellari nemo nostrum ambigit; et quod aeternae vitae promissiones regnumque Coelorum ad novum pertinet Testamentum; sed in illis temporalibus figuras fuisse futurorum quae implerentur in nobis, in quos finis saeculorum obvenit, non suspicio mea, sed Apostolicus intellectus est, dicente Paulo, cum de talibus loqueretur ..."— Augustine, *Contra Faustum*, 4:2, *PL* 42:217-218.

... a relationship between the realities of the Old Testament and those of the New. The great patristic affirmation is that this sense has Christ for its object. The people, the events, and the institutions of the Old Testament have primarily an historical reality of their own which is their literal sense, and secondarily they posses a certain prefiguration of what Christ has accomplished at the end of time.[67]

Thus it is that across the Old Testament one figure is fashioned little by little with a variety of features. The difference between the Old Testament and the New is, as Danielou says, "the difference between Christ represented and Christ present".[68] Many authors have affirmed that the Christological sense, the Christic correspondence, is an essential element in the definition of the type. Typology, according to Richardson, for example, "... is the doctrine that the coming of Jesus Christ and his Church were foreshadowed in the persons and events of the Old Testament".[69]

But the terminology can be deceptive. Danielou himself admits: "The typological sense, then, has for its object only Christ. But it has for its object the whole Christ."[70] This "whole Christ" in Danielou's view contains many actual varieties of type:

... the Christological meaning can be subdivided into as many sections as there are aspects in Christ himself. Christ may be considered either as a historical Person manifested in the events recorded in the Gospel, or living a hidden life in the "sacraments" of the Church which is his body, or as appearing at the parousia at the end of the world and reigning in glory. Further, these three adventus, to use a term of St. Augustine's, have more than one side to them. In the historical Christ we may consider either the external actions of his earthly life or the spiritual content of its mysteries. In the mystical Christ, again, we may consider either the collective aspect, which is the whole Church, or the separate members, each of whom has to "put on" Christ (Romans 13:14; Galatians 3:27).[71]

---

[67] Typology is "... une relation entre les réalités de l'Ancien Testament et celles du Nouveau. La grande affirmation patristique est que ce sens a pour l'objet le Christ. Les personnages, les événements, les institutions de l'Ancien Testament ont premièrement une réalité historique propre qui est leur sens litteral, et, secondement, ils sont une certaine préfiguration de ce que le Christ a accompli à la fin des temps." — Jean Danielou, "Les divers sens de l'Écriture dans la tradition chretienne primitive," *Ephemerides Theologicae Lovanienses*, XXIV (1948), 120.
[68] Danielou, 120.
[69] Richardson, "The Rise of Modern Biblical Scholarship ...", 333. See also Goppelt, *Typos: die typologischen Deutung des alten Testaments im Neuen*, 139.
[70] Danielou, "Les divers sens," 120. See also Burghardt, "On Early Christian Exegesis", 81: "Typology announces the 'Whole Christ'."
[71] Danielou, *Origen*, p. 161. Similarly: "The Christian faith has but one object: the mystery of Christ dead and risen. But this one only mystery subsists under different

It is perhaps deceptive then to insist that all typology must be Christological in any but the widest acceptance of the term. But the concept has
a long history in typological exegesis, and does no real harm as long as
it is properly understood as the "whole Christ" which is in question.

The Christological element in typology is clearly expressed by John
Donne, for example, when he says that Christ is the

> ... subject of the Word of God, of all the Scriptures, of all that was shadowed
> in the Types, and figur'd in the Ceremonies, and prepared in the presentation
> of the Law, of all that was foretold by the Prophets, of all that the Soule of man
> rejoiced in, and congratulated with the spirit of God, in the Psalms, and in the
> Canticles, and in the cheerful parts of spiritual joy and exultation, which we
> have in the Scriptures; Christ is the foundation of all those Scriptures, Christ is
> the burden of all those Songs; Christ was in *sermone* then, then he was in the
> Word.[72]

If the Christic correspondence is properly understood, the notion of
typological recapitulation which has been discussed above, becomes
much more meaningful. For it is Christ alone who recapitulates all things
in himself. As Andrewes says in the seventeenth century, Christ is truly
recapitulative, the first and the last Truth:

> The first and last both. For now by his coming he is the adequation of the
> Word and the Work, the Promise and the Performance. That way he is Truth
> too, the truth of all types, the truth of all Prophecies; for "in Him are all the
> promises yea and Amen," (2 Cor. 1:20) — yes, in the first truth; Amen, in the
> last. The actual verifying is the truth when all is done, and that he is by his
> birth.[73]

Whether typology must be strictly Christological or not is a disputed
point and much involved in terminology. The Fathers certainly did not
express themselves in the terminology used by contemporary scholars
such as Danielou. Nor did they use the many categories common in
contemporary exegetical practice. They were far simpler in their approach
to scripture. It is perhaps unfair then to impose modern terms and categories on the patristic interpretation of typology. But even in the
Fathers, there is no doubt that the divine relevance, Christological or

---

modes. It is prefigured in the Old Testament; it is realized historically in the life of
Christ on earth; it is contained by way of mystery in the sacraments; it is lived mysti-
cally in souls; it is accomplished socially in the Church; it is consummated eschatalogi-
cally in the kingdom of heaven. Thus the Christian has at his disposal, for the expression of that single reality, several registers, a symbolism of several dimensions." —
J. Danielou, "Le symbolisme du Baptisme", *Dieu Vivant*, I (1947), 17.

[72] Donne, *Sermons*, ed. Potter and Simpson, I, 287–288.

[73] Lancelot Andrewes, *Sermons on the Nativity* (Grand Rapids, Michigan, 1955), 182.

not, is an essential element of typology. This is the point which must be emphasized. The typological structure is utterly dependent upon God's working and acting in history.

The whole biblical history is the result of the continuous impact of the un-changing God upon the life of his people and it would be surprising indeed if the essential pattern of his dealings with men were not visible throughout. This is the philosophy upon which typology is based. The great crucial events of biblical history — the Creation, the Judgment upon Adam and the men of Noah's generation, the Salvation of men by the Ark or Exodus, the establish-ment of the saving Covenants, the choice of a "Peculiar" People — exhibit in unmistakable fashion the way God works.[74]

6. CONCLUSION

A passage from William Lynch summarizes the discussion thus far on the nature and definition of typology and its four constituent elements:

In the first place there are the literal words of the biblical text. As St. Thomas insists, the function of words in the Bible is the same as in any other book. They are the signs of things, of realities other than themselves, and the referential meaning is to be gathered from the text itself and from the context. But uniquely in the case of the Bible and this because of God's structural governance of supernatural history, the realities signified by the text have a referential relationship to other realities in history. The Jews of the Old Testament are liberated from Egypt and from the waters of the Red Sea. This is more than a word, it is also an historical fact. Yet without becoming less of a fact, it is also a sign, a type, of another reality to come, the liberation of Christ from the dead. Yet it is more than an historical metaphor, or an artificial sign implanted in a fact, chosen at random to be related to something else. For it has the same concrete structure, though on a poorer and less important level, as that greater thing toward which it points. And the deeper one goes into the whole historical concretion of the earlier reality, the more insight there is into that which is to come (reality is no block to insight, as it is to so many forms of the romantic imagination). But the reverse is also true. If one brings the Resurrection back over against the liberation of the ancient people from the waters, that first act of liberation is illuminated as never before. There is a mutuality of forces for insight operating between the two events. Each is borrowing light from the other. Just when our insight is losing contact with the reality of one, we have the wherewithal to restore the vision through the other. We can imagine as God imagined, as He drew his people from the waters. He is already carving out the forms of his Son according to all the possibilities of different historical materials. Yet the mate-rials keep their full historical identity. God's imagination is not universal.[75]

[74] Dentan, "Typology — Its Use and Abuse", 212-213. See also Markus, "Presup-positions ...", 81.
[75] William F. Lynch, S.J., *Christ and Apollo*, 188-189.

It is obvious that this whole notion of typology, and each one of its four essential elements, depends most significantly upon a world view, a theology of history that is distinctly and uniquely biblical. In the following chapter, therefore, an attempt shall be made to outline this basic theological view of history which underlies and illuminates all the essential elements of typology.

IV

TYPOLOGY AND HISTORY

> Typology gives expression to the specific intelligibility that belongs to history as such. Without it, the events recorded would convey no assimilable meaning to our bewildered comprehension; the key is the possibility of reference back to earlier manifestations of the same ways.
>
> Danielou, *The Lord of History*, p. 6.

It is obvious that the notion of typology rests upon a clearly conceived view of history that is uniquely biblical, and each one of the essential elements of the typological structure is meaningless without this framework of biblical history to support it. Typological realism, the metaphysical correspondence of type and antitype, and the evolutionary development of the antitype as *forma perfectior*, demand a framework and a context of history which is able to explain and clarify these elements. It is clear, for example, that Paul's typological interpretations, as well as the exegesis of the Fathers, contain the "seed of a philosophy of history".[1] Perhaps it would be more accurate to call it a theology of history, because the uniquely biblical view of history transcends purely natural and secondary causes and demands the intervention of the divine. It is the fourth element of typology, the relevance of the divine, which essentially characterises the biblical view of history which is the basis of all typology.

1. THE RELEVANCE OF GOD IN HISTORY

At the basis of this typological history is the undeniable belief that God exists and is operative in all the actions of human beings and of nature itself. Without this theology of history and this providential view of the world, typology becomes mere metaphor and loses all historical meaning.[2]

[1] Joseph Anthony Mazzeo, *Medieval Cultural Tradition In Dante's Comedy* (Ithaca, New York: Cornell University Press, 1960), 176.
[2] For a comprehensive bibliography of Theology and History, see G. Thils, "La théologie de l'histoire: Note Bibliographique", *Ephemerides Theologicae Lovanienses*,

Both the type and the antitype must be fitted into a biblical and historical frame of reference. This implies that every historical occurrence is at the same time a part of a larger world view, part of a much larger historical context which reaches both beyond and above the individual historical phenomena. Each historical event is thus related to every other event and becomes part of a larger fabric of meaning which elevates individual events while leaving their own historical context untouched.

The principal of Divine Relevance means that God acts in history. "According to the traditional Christian view of the world", Case says, "God makes history. He stands at the beginning and at the end of time; and in the intervening area, when the course of temporal events is being shaped, providential guidance is continually operative. This is the major premise on which the older Christian interpretation of history is based."[3] Meaning is given to history because God uses the temporal events of human and historical life to teach and to lead mankind towards the eternal city.

The man of the Old Testament knows nothing of an order of nature, governed by law, comprehensible in terms of rational thought. But he believes in a God who has created the world and gives it unto the charge of man as the place for his dwelling and working. Man conceives God as the ruler of history, who directs the historical process to a goal in accordance with his plan. Therefore he is sure that there is an order in all occurrences although not one which is intelligible to reason. Certainly human life is weak, fragile and ephemeral, but the word of God stands unshaken and man can rely on it.[4]

The prophets and writers of the Old Testament saw a definite plan in history. They believed that all history was in the hands of God, and that the whole of history was subject to God's providential will. Human history, therefore, is a part of God's consciousness. Thorlief Boman points out the importance of this notion of Divine Consciousness in biblical history:

It is clear what meaning God's consciousness must have had for the Hebrews; the life of man encompasses a small part of the history of existence, the life of a people a greater part, the life of humanity a still greater part, but the life of

---

XXVI (1950), 87-95 and *Répertoire Bibliographique de la Philosophie*, 5, Louvain (February, 1953), 135 and (August, 1953), 392. Supplementary to these articles and covering the period 1948-1953 is Charles P. Loughran, "Theology and History: A Bibliography", *Thought*, XXIX (1954), 101-115. See also the bibliography compiled by W. Norris Clark, S.J., in the *News of the Institute for the Religious and Social Studies Fellowship*, 3800 Broadway, New York 27, New York, for November, 1953. For the medieval conception of history see Henri De Lubac, *Exégèse Médiévale*, I, 425-487.

[3] Shirley Jackson Case, *The Christian Philosophy of History* (Chicago: University of Chicago Press, 1943), 14.

[4] D. Rudolf Bultmann, *History and Eschatology* (Edinburgh: The University Press, 1957), 6-7.

God encompasses everything. God's consciousness is a world consciousness in which everything that takes place is treasured and held fast in the eternal and is therefore as indestructible as "matter". Without a world consciousness, all the history of humanity and of the universe would end in nothing; for a people, however, for whom life and history is everything, the concept of a divine world consciousness is as necessary as the concept of eternal being was for the Greeks. For the Israelites, the world was transitory, but Jehovah and his words (and deeds) were eternal (Isaiah 40:8).[5]

God's providential control of history is a concept that has very little meaning for us today, but it was still very real in the seventeenth century. Because of this providence of God man was "surrounded and supported by the divine order which rules in nature and History".[6] God acts in history and reveals himself in history. "Or rather", as De Lubac points out, "God inserts himself in history and so bestows on it a 'religious consecration' which compels us to treat it with due respect."[7] Because of this divine insert in history, historical happenings are changed. A new dimension is added to them; they become *events*, more than mere occurrences.

Thus the deliverance of Israel at the Red Sea might have been "explained" on purely rational grounds as the result of a wind sweeping across the desert and piling up the waters before it, and this is actually suggested in Exodus 14:11; but it became an event in the life and destiny of Israel and changed the course of their history, because the prophet Moses saw its deeper significance for faith, discovered the dimensions of eternity within it and interpreted it as an act of God whereby the people were delivered from their enemies.[8]

In other words, the Exodus is the manifestation of God's providential care of his people, and it takes its place in a long chain of events governed by God so as to work out his plan of salvation among men.

History is, therefore, not merely a succession of heterogeneous events. It constitutes a divine plan. Every stage in the evolution of that divine plan represents an advance on its predecessors, but also a continuation of them. Only in this way does history become an intelligible process, and a constant revelation of the providential guidance of God at every moment of that history. History, then, becomes operative on two levels. It is not

[5]   Thorlief Boman, *Hebrew Thought Compared With Greek*, trans. Jules L. Moreau (Philadelphia: The Westminster Press, 1960), 139.
[6]   Bultmann, 7. On Christian Providence, see for example Etienne Gilson, *The Spirit of Medieval Philosophy*, trans. A. H. C. Downes (New York: Charles Scribners' Sons, 1940), Chapter VIII, 148-167.
[7]   Henri De Lubac, S.J., *Catholicism*, trans. Lancelot C. Sheppard (New York: Sheed and Ward, 1958), 83.
[8]   E. C. Rust, *The Christian Understanding of History* (London: Lutterworth Press, 1947), 69.

only "a series of historical events" but it is also a series of events in which "God himself acts in order to disclose and actualize his purpose in the lives of men". The events encompass a deeper meaning; they are "pregnant with divine meaning and therefore not mere occurrences". The true meaning of historical existence "is disclosed by God only to faith, for this meaning is concerned with the sovereign purpose of a personal God".[9]

Hence history may be said to have an eternal significance — that is, significance in and for eternity. For it is genuinely part of the eternal counsel of God, called into being by his creative power, grounded in his providential wisdom, and transfigured by his redeeming grace. Thus history is neither a treadmill of meaningless recurrences nor a pattern of so-called "timeless" moments but a living fabric of continuous influences ....[10]

2. TIME AND ETERNITY

Most western concepts of history picture time as a straight line upon which we stand, as Boman points out, looking forward. The future is in front of us and the past is behind us. On this line of history, we can define all tenses by determined points. The present is the point at which we are standing; the future is at some point in front of us, the past is behind us, and the pluperfect still further behind us.[11] Events exist in a historical sequence on a horizontal line moving always toward some distant point in the future. Each point can be defined by the events that precede it, and each event is a further definition and clarification of those that precede it.

But in the typological view of history, the meaning comes not from the horizontal, but vertically from above. The notion of divine relevance, of God's providence shaping events in history, adds a vertical dimension to all of history. Thus Shirley Case can speak with justice of God being "within, as well as above the universe", of the "insert from God out of eternity", of "eternity impinging on time" or of "the entry into history of a reality from beyond history — by a creative act of God vertically from above".[12]

There are these intrusions of eternity into time ... Each such intrusion is both a historical reality and a premise. While for secular historiography the immediate fact is regarded as secure and the interpretation is naturally incomplete, in

---

[9] Rust, 21.
[10] Roger Hazelton, "Time, Eternity, and History", *The Journal of Religion*, XXX (January, 1950), 11.
[11] Boman, *Hebrew Thought Compared With Greek*, 124.
[12] Case, *The Christian Philosophy of History*, 210, 117. Rust, 69 speaks of the "dimension of eternity".

figuralism [typology] the general interpretation is given through revelation and
the dates are subject to it not only for interpretation but even for selection.
Each event possesses an archetypal meaning whose fulfillment lies in the mind
of God ... They are not only preparatory and prospective of temporal events
but are preparatory of the eternal and otherworldly, pointing not only forward
to the future but "upward" to eternity, where they already exist as complete
in the mind of God. Time is thus the moving image of eternity.[13]

This type of interpretation obviously introduces a whole new concept of
history. The Greco-Roman concept of history, as basically linear or
cyclic, is essentially horizontal and spatial, if such terms may be used to
describe a temporal dimension. The Christian biblical concept of history,
because of the essential relevance of the divine, is vertical, and in a sense,
essentially, non-spatial. The typological interpretation establishes a link
between events which cannot be adequately explained on the horizontal
plane. The events, as Auerbach points out so often, are linked neither
temporally nor causally. The relationship between the two events can be
established only if the two events of the typological structure are linked
vertically to divine providence,

... which alone is able to devise such a plan of history and supply the key to its
understanding. The horizontal, that is, the temporal and the causal, connection
of occurrences is dissolved; the here and now is no longer a mere link in an
earthly chain of events, it is simultaneously something which has always been,
and which will be fulfilled in the future; and strictly, in the eyes of God, it is
something eternal, something omni-temporal, something already consummated
in the realm of fragmentary earthly events.[14]

Operating on the horizontal plane, secular historians can explain to a
certain extent every historical fact by its immediate cause, and they can
foresee, within limits, its immediate consequences. But the typological
view of history is essentially incomplete on this level. The full meaning
of all historical events must be sought beyond the horizontal. We must
look for the ultimate meaning of events on the vertical plane of God's
intrusion into time from out of eternity.

It is in this way that an understanding of history can be reached which
is essentially biblical and Christian. Hazelton points out so well:

Such an understanding depends upon a perspective in which time and eternity
are conceived together, as relevantly and meaningfully conjoined, not simply
held apart by means of theological antitheses. A Christian ... sees history as
the very juncture of time and eternity, trusts profoundly in the God who works

---

[13]   Mazzeo, *Medieval Cultural Tradition in Dante's Comedy*, 178.
[14]   Auerbach, *Mimesis*, 64-65.

eternally to reconcile the temporal order to himself, and hopes even against hope for the final victory of God's eternal purpose over, yet also within, the passing drift and flux of time.[15]

This brings us to the final point, which is the eternal contemporaneity of God at every moment of temporal history. Rust defines the concept by saying:

Because the dimension of eternity is hidden within the event of Jesus Christ, He is contemporaneous with every moment of time and through His Holy Spirit still confronts men in their own concrete historical situation. He is not shut up in the historical past (nor I might add in the historical future) but breaks down all the barriers of space and time. The act of salvation wrought in history is present at every instant of the subsequent (and antecedent) time process.[16]

Speaking of this eternal contemporaneity, Boman says that "To be a true Christian and truly believe in Christ ... means to leap across and forget the centuries in order to become contemporaneous with Jesus".[17]

This is exactly the notion that Milton was able to convey in his poem on the Nativity. Milton immediately establishes the note of contemporaneity in the opening lines of that poem:

> This is the month and this the happy morn
> Wherein the Son of Heav'n's eternal King,
> Of Wedded Maid, and Virgin Mother born,
> Our great redemption from above did bring.
> (ll. 1-4)[18]

With the skilful manipulation of past and present tenses, and the careful juxtaposition of past and present events, Milton maintains the tone of an event past and completed, yet still immediate and operative in the present.

> That glorious form ...
> ...
> He laid aside ...
> Forsook the Courts of everlasting Day
> And chose with us a darksome House of Clay.
> (ll. 8-14)

The sense of simultaneity in past and present is further underlined by the use of paradoxical images throughout the poem: "Wedded Maid, and Virgin Mother" (l. 3), "Glorious Form" and "Mortal Clay" (ll. 8, 14).

[15] Hazelton, "Time, Eternity, and History", 1.
[16] Rust, *The Christian Understanding of History*, 50.
[17] Boman, *Hebrew Thought Compared with Greek*, 147-148.
[18] All Milton references are to Merritt Y. Hughes, ed., *John Milton: Complete Poems and Major Prose* (New York: Odyssey Press, 1957).

The Hymn itself begins in the past:

> It was the Winter wild
> (l. 29)

and

> ... peaceful was the night
> Wherein the Prince of Light
> His reign of peace upon the earth began.
> (ll. 61-63)

and

> The shepherds on the lawn,
>
> ...
>
> Sat simply chatting in a rustic row.
> (ll. 85-87)

Yet alternately, Milton pictures the event as present.

> ... Birds of calm sit brooding on the charmed wave.
> (l. 68)

and

> The stars with deep amaze
> Stand fixt in steadfast gaze.
> (ll. 69-70)

The biblical event in Milton's poem is past and accomplished, and yet strangely present:

> The Babe lies yet in smiling Infancy,
> That on the bitter cross
> Must redeem our loss;
> (ll. 151-153)
>
> ...
>
> And then at last our bliss
> Full and perfect is,
> But now begins; for from this happy day
> (ll. 165-167)
>
> ...
>
> The oracles are dumb ...
> (l. 173)

The event is brought meaningfully present and contemporaneous in the magnificent final stanza of the poem:

> But see! The virgin blest
> Hath laid her Babe to rest.
> Time is our tedious song should here have ending:

Heav'n's youngest-teemed Star
Hath fixt her polished Car,
Her sleeping Lord with Handmaid Lamp attending:
And all about the Courtly stable
Bright-harness'd Angels sit in order serviceable.

(ll. 237-244)

Milton's hymn almost literally leaps across and forgets the centuries in order to become contemporaneous with the biblical event. The immediacy of the event for Milton is achieved through the contemporaneity of time and of presence. The event is present, not past, and the poet is a participant in the scene. He is actually present from dawn to dusk as the event occurs in the past, yet strangely present. A similar approach can be seen in Milton's poem *Upon the Circumcision*, and to a lesser degree in *The Passion*. The contemporaneity of the past historical occurrence in the present liturgical event, which is Milton's basis for these poems, is essentially typological and based upon the vertical relevance of God and the meeting of time and eternity in the biblical and liturgical event.[19] This contemporaneity is somehow missing in Crashaw's Hymn, *In the Holy Nativity of Our Lord God: A Hymn Sung as by the Shepherds*, where the hymn itself is sung by shepherds and the poet is not immediately present. Also all tenses are past, the event is over and done with and spoken of as a completed historical act. The sense of immediacy is lost. Similarly in Ben Jonson's *A Hymne on the Nativitie of My Saviour*. There are no intermediate shepherds but the event is past tense:

I sing the birth, was borne tonight
The Author both of Life, and Light.

Milton's poem is a much clearer reflection of the contemporaneity of events in the Christian view of divinely relevant history. It is this same notion of divine contemporaneity, reflected in Milton's *Nativity Hymn*, which gives meaning to Thomas Browne's passage:

Before Abraham was, I am, is the saying of Christ; yet is it true in some sense, if I say it of myself; For I was not only before myself, but Adam, that is in the Idea of God, and the decree of the Synod held from all eternity. And in this sense, I say, the World was before the creation, and at an end before it had a beginning; and thus was I dead before I was alive: though my grave be England.

---

[19] See also Milton's "On Time" and Sonnet VII, "How Soon Hath Time". Also Lawrence Stapleton, "Milton's Conception of Time in the Christian Doctrine", *Harvard Theological Review*, LVII (1964), 9-21. There is a discussion of Milton's use of tenses in the *Nativity Ode* in Lowry Nelson, Jr., *Baroque Lyric Poetry* (New Haven and London: Yale University Press, 1961), 32-34, 41-51. I believe that we can go one step beyond Nelson's discussion and discover the reason for Milton's sense of contemporaneity in the *Nativity Ode* in the patterns of biblical and liturgical typology.

my dying place was Paradise: and Eve miscarried of me before she conceived of Cain.[20]

3. CHRISTIAN HISTORY

Christian history, therefore, is the earthly reflection of God's divine plan, the execution of God's eternal intentions in the historical context of time. The Bible, in its turn, becomes the record of this Christian history, the written chronicle of God's dealings with men. God is everywhere present and operative in the Bible, just as he is in history. Such a view of history emphasizes three main elements in the analysis of God's dealings with men.[21]

First and foremost, the providential view of history underlines the importance of the individual event in the course of history. Because each event represents the intersection of time and eternity, the insertion of God within the framework of historical time, it becomes much more than just an occurrence. It carries an added weight of divine relevance. It is difficult, if not impossible, to assess God's presence in a mere symbol, whereas God's presence in a real event can be measured and understood. The event, then, becomes increasingly more important in the plan of God's salvation. For:

God's plan of salvation cannot otherwise be spoken of than by reference to definite points in time, which by their special significance stand out from the ordinary course of events in bold relief and become landmarks of God's progressive action towards the attainment of his purpose. The delivery from Egypt, the sealing of the Covenant at Sinai, the conquest of the Promised Land are named at the very beginning of God's relation with Israel as the decisive points in the course of events, to which the people's thinking is to be directed in order to understand the more recent acts of God and to face them in proper readiness. For again and again in the course of history such times and days of Jehovah appear, announced by seer and prophet, expected and lived through in suspense because God's hidden redemptive will appears and provides a new goal for the work begun.[22]

[20]   Sir Thomas Browne, *Religio Medici*, Everyman Edition (New York: E.P. Dutton and Company, Inc., 1951), 65-66.
[21]   For the inspiration of the following remarks I am indebted to J. Danielou, *The Lord of History*, trans. Nigel Abercrombie (London: Longmans, 1958), and "The Conception of History in the Christian Tradition", *The Journal of Religion*, XXX (July, 1950), 171-179. However, I have modified some of Danielou's views and perhaps have gone beyond his original intention. The connection of his remarks with the essential constituents of typology is my own.
[22]   Walter Eichrodt, *Theologische Zeitschrift*, XXX (1956), 103. The translation is by Jules Moreau in Boman, *Hebrew Thought Compared With Greek*, 141-142.

The Bible is the record of these significant events — the covenant with Abraham, the Exodus, the Sacrifice of Isaac, the Flood. God's plan can be traced and followed in these events, for each of them represents a new stage in the actualization of God's plan. Each one of these events represents, in a sense, a καίρος, a moment of decision, a fullness of time, a pivotal point in the history of growth. Each event is also a new beginning, different, and yet not completely alien to all that has gone before it. It represents a new beginning that is still a continuation, because it marks just one further step in the fulfillment of the whole divine plan. Thus Gregory of Nyssa can speak of Christian history as "beginning from beginning to beginning, by successive beginnings that have no end".[23] This is the significance and the value of the individual event in the history of salvation.

It is a notion that is difficult for us to understand. As Boman says:

We ... must learn to regard events as facts that are and abide. The sound waves that mediate the melody to us disperse (as indeed all light waves, too, vanish, or are turned into heat), but the melody itself lingers and never perishes for us, as psychology teaches us. In a similar way significant historical events remain indestructible facts in the life of a people. The consequences of the events can be altered in a positive or negative direction by new deeds or failures, but the events themselves can never be altered; they belong to the permanent stock of the people's life. If this is the actual state of affairs regarding what has happened, we understand that the difference between past and present is less important than the qualitative distinction between events; a decisive event of antiquity can balance many current events in the evaluation of the present.[24]

This is certainly true of Christian history. It is indeed determined by one single event which sums up and outweighs all other events which either prefigure or look back to it. This pivotally significant event is the Incarnation, which is exactly what Cullman has tried to say in *Christ and Time*, underlining the importance of the Resurrection.[25] But just as this one great event, the insertion of Christ, Son of God, into the framework of historical time, has altered history, so in a limited degree has each one of the typological events that led up to it. The Covenant, Adam, and the Exodus are individual events of extreme importance in the course of biblical and Christian history. It is the event which determines the sub-

[23] *In Cantica Canticorum, Homilia, X, PG* 44:981c.
[24] Boman, 138.
[25] Oscar Cullmann, *Christ and Time*, trans. Floyd V. Filson (Philadelphia: Westminster Press, 1950).

sequent direction of history insofar as it is a partial revelation of God's progressive plan of salvation.[26]

History, however, is much more than the chronicle of events. It demands a certain succession of events, which is the second important element in the Christian view of history — the notion of continuity, linking the individual events together. As seen through Christian eyes, the second distinctive characteristic of history is the "organic interconnection of its successive stages".[27] This element, as has been seen above, is clearly manifested in the typological interpretation of biblical history as the metaphysical correspondence of type and antitype. As Tresmontant points out:

History is not an eternal flow of unrelated events. It has a beginning (bereschit), and is ordered to an end, just as the tree's growth is ordered to fruitfulness. And so in this maturation of history there are *stages*: "times" and "moments".

It is characteristic of biblical history that those who carry it forward are made aware of its *direction* through the teaching of the prophets. The prophet, the *nabi*, is someone who understands the "sense" of history, what it means and whither it moves ... An historical event is a *sign* only insofar as one may read in it what will come of it, just as we can foretell, when the bud appears, that the flower will follow. It is not because of some extrinsic relationship, but very simply because the former actuality does produce the latter. The *nabi* is aware of God's creative action and understands those "phases" of it which regard man especially. In this he is like the farmer who knows the "time" of the maturation of his crops. "The King turned to the wise men who had knowledge of the times." (Esther 1:13). "A knowledge of the times to determine what Israel should do." (1 Chronicles 12:33).

But the prophet does not see history stretched out before him like a map, from which he need only pick out individual future events. Such foresight is not the prophet's gift. Rather he sees in which direction events are flowing. This is the scope of prophecy. The Hebrew conception of time excludes any other explanation of it.

It is in the New Testament that we find this awareness of creative time, this sense of the moments of maturation most accurately expressed. "The time is fulfilled ... the kingdom of God is at hand." (Mark 1:15).[28]

The organic relationship of events in the flow of Christian and divine providential history received its definite formulation in the works of Gregory of Nyssa.[29] Gregory characterizes God's plan and its gradual evolution in history as ἀκολούθια, which he defines as succession, con-

---

[26]   See also Lynch's chapter on the importance of the Definite in Christian History and Theology, *Christ and Apollo*, Chapter I, 3-30.

[27]   Danielou, *The Lord of History*, 241.

[28]   Claude Tresmontant, *A Study of Hebrew Thought*, 27.

[29]   See Danielou, *The Lord of History*, Chapter VI, 241ff.

tinuity, the evolutionary idea of before and after, the gradual unfolding of God's plan through all its phases.

... God established in one and the same instant, all at once, the principles, the potentialities, and the causes of all things, which were thus brought into existence from the first act of his creative will ... but the power and the wisdom bestowed on them were elicited through a chain of accentuation, so that each constituent part of the whole should be brought to its perfection in one order ... Things come forth in their turn, each one as a necessary consequence of the former, according to the laws of nature's workmanship, throughout the whole chain of succession. (ἀκολούθια).[30]

This principle of ἀκολούθια is operative on the natural order, on the level of human nature, and also on the level of historical development.[31]

Gregory's teaching represents one of the most determined attempts that have been made to enucleate the structural principles of the development of the history of salvation on the full scale, that is embracing the totality of history. St. Augustine's comparable work in the *City of God* ... is quite unlike it. If one had to compare the two, one could say that Augustine is more concerned with the divine initiative, Gregory with the free human response. These attitudes reflect the general trends of Western and Eastern theology; from the point of view of the theandric synergism which we have recognized as part of the inwardness of history, they represent complementary systems, each emphasizing one of the two inseparable aspects of the case.[32]

Danielou points out that in the historical context of a maturing Christian theology, the controversy with Greek philosophy emphasized the first aspect of the Christian view of history, the importance of single events. The controversy with Jewish thought focused attention on the second aspect of this vision of history, "the nature of the link which gives these events unity among themselves". For history demands not only that events have importance, but there must be a continuity between them as well. In Christian history, the individual event is inserted "into the web of an economy which goes beyond" the individual event and "which constitutes an objective plan".[33]

This vision is one of progressive economy. The Old and the New Testaments enter into a single plan but represent two successive moments of it. For Irenaeus the reason for this progression is of a pedagogical nature. Everything which is in time must begin in a state of imperfection. (*Adv. Haer.* iv: 11:22).

[30] *PG* 44:72 b-c.
[31] *De Mortuis, PG* 46:517d: *De anima et resurrectione, PG* 46:105a; *De Hominis opificio, PG* 44:236b, c: *Contra Eunomium*, I, *PG* 45:364c, 365a, 369b, 433d.
[32] Danielou, *The Lord of History*, 251, 252.
[33] Danielou, "The Conception of History in the Christian Tradition", 172.

God does not share this imperfection. Before the full manifestation to his people, he began by accustoming them to his ways, by educating them. (*Adv. Haer.*, 9:1). Thus it is that he led them from secondary things to primary things, from types to relatives, from the temporal to the eternal, from the carnal to the spiritual, from the earthly to the heavenly. (*Adv. Haer.*, 14:3).[34]

Donne echoes this view of Christian History in many places, especially in his sermons. In a sermon on 1 Timothy 1:15 preached on April 19, 1618, he wrote:

... when God comes to speak at first in the Old Testament though he came to more particulars, yet it was in dark speeches, and in vails; and to them who understood best, and saw clearest into God's word, still it was but *de futura*, by way of promise, and of a future thing ... the Old Testament is but a preparation and a pedagogie to the New.[35]

History, however, is not an unending series of interrelated, continuous events. History, by definition, is not eternity. History must come to an end, and this is the third and final essential concept in the Christian view of history — the emphasis and importance of the end of time, the ἔσχατον. The two categories of event and of progress or continuity do not exhaust the concept of Christian history. If they did, the result would be a history capable of infinitely reproducing itself and continuing on into the indefinite future. "Any such view", as Danielou remarks so well, "would leave out of account the further essential truth, that Christianity is not only progress, but itself the goal of progress. This third and final characteristic of the Christian outlook on history is its eschatalogical quality; the idea of an end, an ἔσχατον, is of capital importance in the system."[36] Christian history, therefore, is not conceived of as an indefinite progress, but as definitely finite. It is determined and circumscribed. It points always towards the End. It is difficult to overlook this emphasis on the ἔσχατον in the early Christian Church. The whole life of the Church is tempered by this constant reference to the Eschaton, the moment when Christ will come in glory, the fulfillment of all types and shadows.

4. TYPOLOGY AND THE THEOLOGY OF HISTORY

These three categories then, the Kairos, the Akolouthia, and the Eschaton, which form the heart of the Christian approach to history are the

[34] "The Conception of History ...", 173.
[35] John Donne, *The Sermons*, ed. Potter and Simpson, I, 291.
[36] Danielou, *The Lord of History*, 6-7.

same three elements which stand as the foundation upon which any meaningful typological interpretation of scripture is to be built. The importance and the historical reality of the event, the Kairos, the typical or antitypical term in the typological relationship, has already been discussed at some length, as has the metaphysical correspondence which fits both terms of the typological relationship into a continuing movement of growth, of progress, of Akolouthia. If the typological structure is carried out to the three term relationship used by many of the Fathers, the Eschaton is the complete fulfillment of the New Testament Antitype, which in its turn is a *forma perfectior* of the Old Testament type. Both Old Testament type and New Testament antitype are Kairoi, events which carry a divine meaning. Their complete fulfillment in the evolution of the divine Akolouthia is most perfectly achieved at the end of all time and Akolouthia, in the moment of the Eschaton.

Typology, then, is not an exegesis of the books of the Old Testament; it is rather an interpretation of the history itself which these books recount. It establishes connections between the events of the two histories. This means that typology is concerned only with those events in which the divine relevance is clearly manifested. The great error of the allegorical exegesis of the Alexandrians was that it sought to find meanings hidden in all the texts of scripture. Traditional typology recognizes only those special relationships which are the "sacraments" of scripture, and which are charged with a theological significance which helps us to understand the sense of certain mysteries of Christ. While at the same time the mysteries of Christ throw a retrospective light back over these relationships themselves.[37]

In similar fashion Auerbach speaks of the "method of revisional interpretation of history" which revises, in a certain sense, the historical events in the light of figural and typological interpretation. The actual historical events of the Old Testament have an added emphasis when viewed in the light of typology, and the "sensory occurrence pales before the power of the figural meaning".[38]

Typology is actually the relationship which unites the Old and the

---

[37] "La typologie n'est donc pas ... une exégèse des livres de l'ancien Testament; elle est une interprétation de l'histoire même que ces livres racontent. Elle établit des liaisons entre les événements des deux histoires. C'est dire également qu'elle ne porte que sur les événements où cette action divine se manifeste. Ce sera la grande erreur de l'exégèse allégorique d'Alexandrie, de vouloir chercher des sens cachés a tous les textes de l'Écriture. La typologie traditionelle connait seulement des lieux privilegées, qui sont les "sacrements" de l'Écriture, et qui sont chargés d'une signification théologique qui nous aide à comprendre le sens de certains mystères du Christ en même temps que les mystères du Christ jettent sur eux une lumière rétrospective." — J. Danielou, "La typologie d'Isaac dans le Christianisme Primitif", *Biblica*, XXVIII (1947), 369.
[38] Auerbach, *Mimesis*, 42-43.

New Testaments and the final eschatalogical end of all time. Typology unites them both negatively and positively, underlining their similarities and their differences, and emphasizing the growing perfection of the one over the other. Thus it can be said that the Flood, the Resurrection of Christ, Christian Baptism, and the final Judgment where the just will be marked with the blood of the Lamb, all show a fundamental structural analogy. In all of them, God's judgment destroys a sinful man, the old man, the less perfect man, and a new man, the just man, is spared to be the beginning and principle of a new humanity.[39] It is in these momentous and significant Kairoi, divine events — the call of Abraham, the deliverance of Israel through the Exodus, the words of the Prophets, and above all in the life, death and resurrection of Christ and his coming glory at the Eschaton — that the true meaning of Christian history, God's salvific plan, is disclosed. Danielou rightly concludes: "Thus typology expresses the inherent intelligibility of history. It keeps events, where the ways of God are manifested, from being absolutely disconcerting by permitting us to refer them to former manifestations of these same ways."[40]

The Bible, then, presents universal history. It begins with the beginning of time, with creation, and it will end with the Eschaton, the last days when the covenant will be fulfilled and the world will come to an end. Everything else that happens in the world can only find genuine significance as an element in this progressive revelation of God's redeeming plan. "Interpretation in a determined direction", Auerbach says, "becomes a general method of comprehending reality."

In this light the history of no epoch ever has the practical self-sufficiency which, from the standpoint both of primitive man and of modern science, resides in the accomplished fact; all history, rather, remains open and questionable, points to something still concealed, and the tentativeness of events in the figural [typological] interpretation is fundamentally different from the tentativeness of events in the modern view of historical development ... in the figural [typological] system the interpretation is always sought from above, events are considered not in their unbroken relation to one another, but torn apart, individually, each in relation to something other, that is promised and not yet present.[41]

This is an entirely new and uniquely biblical view of history. History becomes "a reality at once continuous and discontinuous" in which there is "a true qualitative difference between past and present and

---

[39] See J. Danielou, "Deluge, baptême, jugement", *Dieu Vivant*, VIII (1947), 97 ff.
[40] Danielou, "The Conception of History in the Christian Tradition", 173. See also *The Lord of History*, 6.
[41] Auerbach, *Mimesis*, 13, and "Figura", 58.

nevertheless an entire ensemble of correspondences and prefigurations".[42] This is true because it is the direction and the meaning which God has impressed upon history. It is this biblical view of history which is at the basis of all genuine typology.

---

[42] J. Danielou, "A Dialogue with Time", *Cross Currents*, I (Winter, 1951), 80. The translation is by Bernard Gilligan.

V

TYPOLOGY IN SEVENTEENTH-CENTURY LITERATURE

> All these things that we read of as having been foretold
> and fulfilled in the past, are still being done under our
> eyes in the present.
>
> Augustine, *De Cat. Rudibus*, 45.

The theology of history which has been outlined in the preceding chapter
is not restricted to the Bible. It forms the basis of all Christian thinking
through the Middle Ages and up to the period under discussion, for the
seventeenth century believed firmly that sacred history did not end with
the final verse of St. John's *Apocalypse*, but was still going on. The very
nature of John's supratemporal visions in that work form the basis of
this view of continuing sacred history, for God's work of salvation continues throughout time to the moment of the Eschaton. God still continues to act in history; the relevance of the divine at every moment of
present and future history is still a meaningful and pregnant concept for
the writers of the seventeenth century. The New Heaven and the New
Earth represent a continuing process of typological fulfillment in the
antitypes of contemporary history, as well as in those of the historically
accomplished New Testament.[1] In this way typology continued to
provide a fertile source of imagery for the poets and prose writers of the
seventeenth century.

It is true that the scriptural exegetes throughout the sixteenth and
seventeenth century began to look with suspicion on the excessive
allegorical interpretations of some of the earlier biblical commentators,
but the Reformers' suspicion of allegorical exegesis did not demand the
rejection of all typological interpretation.

Believing the union of typology and philosophical allegory to be an error
introduced by the Alexandrians and perpetuated by the Schoolmen, they
attempted to renew the pure typology of the New Testament and particularly
of the Pauline Epistles. The scope which Protestant exegetes allowed themselves

---

[1] Apocalypse, 21:1ff.

for such criticism varied considerably, but all were willing to admit that many scriptural passages must be understood typically.[2]

Reformation scriptural exegesis almost universally held one literal sense of scripture, but that one literal sense was often a compound sense, including both the historical and the typical sense.[3]

This compound interpretation, which included the typological world view of the Bible, was not something alien to the reader of the seventeenth century, even in literary works. The audience which watched the plays of Shakespeare and his successors, or at least the more serious minded among them, were accustomed to seeing the "spirit in the letter" everywhere.[4] According to Renaisssance theory, the epic poem was to be interpreted on several levels and the narrative events of the poem could have many levels. It is seen in the early Greek interpretations of the *Iliad* and *Odyssey*, and perhaps finds its most succinct interpretation in Dante's letter to Can Grande. Spenser is very explicit in maintaining that his own poem is to be read in this way, for in his introduction to Raleigh, he feels obliged to comment on how:

... doubtfully all allegories may be construed, and this book of mine, which I have entitled the Faery Queene, being a continued allegory or darke conceit, I have thought good as well for avoyding of gealous opinions and misconstructions, as also for your better light in reading thereof (being so by you commanded) to discover unto you the general intention and meaning, which in the whole course thereof I have fashioned, without expressing of any particular purposes or by accidents therein occasioned.[5]

Apart from the multi-level, spirit and letter interpretation of the epic and other allegorical works in the seventeenth century, strict typological interpretation was very common, and many works, both theological and literary, discussed the typological imagery. In 1588 William Whitaker had published *A Disputation on Holy Scripture* with many references to the typological interpretation of scripture and an analysis of the typological method.[6] In the first quarter of the seventeenth century, John Abbott published *Jesus Prefigured: Or a Poem of the Holy Name of*

[2] H. R. MacCallum, "Milton and the Figurative Interpretation of the Bible", *University of Toronto Quarterly*, XXXI (July, 1962), 404-405.
[3] Milton, *De Doctrine Christiana*, XXX.
[4] Helen Gardner, *The Limits of Literary Criticism*, 40.
[5] *The Poems of Spenser*, ed. J. C. Smith and E. De Selincourt (London: Oxford University Press, 1960), 407.
[6] Translated and edited for the Parker Society by Rev. William Fitzgerald (Cambridge: The University Press, 1849).

Jesus (Antwerp: 1623), which was based on the typological structure of the Old and New Testament. Similar typological parallelism had been used by Christopher Harvey who wrote *Synagogue: Or the Shadow of the Temple* (1640), and John Weemes who published *The Christian Synagogue* at London in 1637. The basic typological view is evident also in works like Thomas Taylor's *Christ Revealed: Or the Old Testament Explained* (1635) and Samuel Mather's *The Figures or Types of the Old Testament* (1683). William Guild's *Moses Unveiled* is a detailed study of the typological relationships between Christ and the Old Testament antitypes — Moses, Adam, Isaac, Aaron, Samson, Joseph, Melchisedech, the Passover, etc., with a listing of the similarities and dissimilarities between type and antitype.[7] Though not explicitly typological, the whole Goodman-Hakewill controversy at the beginning of the seventeenth century on the Providence of God indicates the pertinence of the theological concept of history, and the relevance of the divine in the working out of an ordered plan of salvation which is fundamental to any systematic view of typology.[8]

The literary works of the century also reflect the typological view of scripture and history, although, as MacCallum points out, little has been done to apply the discoveries of scriptural scholars concerning typology to Renaissance and Reformation literature.[9] John Milton, perhaps, is the most obvious example of this typological world-view, which depends upon the compound sense of scripture which he outlined in the *De Doctrina Christiana*.[10] There can be no doubt at all of Milton's indebtedness to scripture throughout his work, and there is no need to belabor his obvious use of the Bible. Sims points out that 1,364 individual citations of Scripture have been recorded by Milton's editors from Hume to Hughes, and Sims himself adds 816 additional references in the two great epics of

---

[7]   William Guild, *Moses Unveiled: Or those Figures which served unto the Pattern and Shadow of Heavenly Things pointing out the Messiah, Christ Jesus briefly explained*, 1620, edited for the Christian Treasury by Rev. T. S. Memes (London: Henry G. Bohn, 1849).
[8]   Godfrey Goodman, *The Fall of Men, or The Corruption of Nature proved by the Light of Natural Reason*, 1616, and George Hakewill, *An Apologie for the Power and Providence of God in the Government of the World*, 1627. The controversy is discussed in R. F. Jones, *Ancients and Moderns* (St. Louis, 1936) and V. Harris, *All Coherence Gone* (Chicago, 1949). For Calvin's views on typology which had such a strong influence on Reformation writers, see R. S. Wallace, *Calvin's Doctrine of Word and Sacrament* (Edinburgh, 1953). For other references to typological interpretation in the seventeenth century, see Joseph H. Summers, "Herbert's Form", *PMLA*, LXVI (1951), 1061-1062.
[9]   MacCallum, "Milton and the Figurative Interpretation of the Bible", footnote 13, p. 414. See also William G. Madsen, *From Shadowy Types to Truth: Studies in Milton's Symbolism* (New Haven: Yale University Press, 1968), Chapter 2.
[10]   Chapter XXX.

Milton.[11] Milton's typological use of scripture is equally clear. In Book V of *Paradise Lost*, Milton has Raphael tell Adam:

> ... and what surmounts the reach of
> Human sense, I shall delineate so,
> By lik'ning spiritual to corporal forms,
> As may express them best, though what if Earth
> Be but the shadow of Heav'n, and things therein
> Each to other like, more than on Earth is thought?[12]

Recent commentators have almost universally interpreted this passage in a Neo-platonic sense,[13] but it would seem that Milton is rather using the word "shadow" in a more strictly typological sense, as a 'foreshadowing' or 'adumbration', and that the imagery of *Paradise Lost* is typological and not necessarily Platonic.[14]

Milton undoubtedly assumed that his readers comprehended the fundamental Christian principles concerning man's part in universal history and his relationship to Christ as the central figure in the divine historical process. The long tradition of typological interpretation in the commentaries and exegesis had firmly established the concept of certain Biblical figures as types foreshadowing Christ ...[15]

Raphael makes this point very clearly in Book XII when he tells Adam that he is presenting the history of mankind by "types and shadows", and speaks of the imperfect Law;

> ... but giv'n
> With purpose to resign them in full time
> Up to a better Cov'nant, disciplin'd
> From shadowy Types to Truth, from Flesh to Spirit.[16]

There have been many attempts to outline the basic structure underlying the "Nativity Ode", but the poem achieves its real force from a basically typological structure. This is corroborated by Milton's manipulation of

---

[11]   James H. Sims, *The Bible in Milton's Epics*, 2-3. See also his exhaustive list of biblical references in Milton, pp. 259-278. Also Harris Francis Fletcher, *The Use of the Bible in Milton's Prose* (Urbana, Ill., University of Illinois Press, 1929) and Fred B. Walker, "Milton's Use of the Bible in His Shorter English Poems", Unpublished MA Thesis, University of Florida, 1947.

[12]   *Paradise Lost*, Book V, ll. 570-575. This particular passage can perhaps throw some light on the confusion that has arisen over the anachronistic and anthropomorphic use of the cannon in the Battle in Heaven in Book VI.

[13]   See for example, the footnote to the passage in the Hughes edition, 315.

[14]   William G. Madsen, "Earth the Shadow of Heaven: Typological Symbolism in *Paradise Lost*", *PMLA*, LXXV (1960), 519.

[15]   Burton O. Kurth, *Milton and Christian Heroism* (Berkeley and Los Angeles: University of California Press, 1959), 8.

[16]   *Paradise Lost*, XII, 232-233, 300-303.

tenses as has been seen in Chapter IV. It seems clear also, that in the first 150 lines of the poem, Milton is presenting a type of the Nativity, and the lines, from l. 150 to the concluding stanza with its neat summary of typological contemporaneity, present the antitype of the first 150 lines in its fulfillment. There are also clear indications of a typological structure in *Upon the Circumcision* and *On the Death of a Fair Infant,* though this latter poem especially is not as successful as the *Nativity Ode* in its expression of a typological mode of thinking. The "righteous sequence of things" (*series justissima rerum*) at the conclusion of *Naturam Non Pati Senium,* is a clear expression of the basic typological structure which Milton sought to reflect in the three great poems at the end of his career.[17] Milton's own conception of his sacred vocation as Poet-Prophet, similar in almost every regard to that of the inspired writer of scripture, confirms his deliberate intention to structure his work on a typological scriptural basis.[18]

Donne's use of typological themes is not as simple as that of Milton, which is not at all unusual considering the difference in the character of the two men, but Donne's typology is as widespread as that of Milton. In the Introduction to *Seventeenth Century Verse and Prose,* White, Wallerstein, and Quintana speak of two basic conceptions helpful to keep in mind while reading Donne. The first is the conception of man as the microcosm reflecting the macrocosm in body and mind, and the second is the "schematic view of the Bible, every event in the Old Testament prefiguring something in the New, as the visible cosmos figures the invisible order".[19] Wallerstein speaks elsewhere of "Donne ... whose imagination is so impregnated with the idea of the symbolic anticipation of the New Testament in the Old".[20] Donne's sermons are very rich in the use of typology, although one must beware of imposing contemporary categories and terminology upon Donne. Like many of the earlier Fathers, Donne himself did not distinguish allegory and typology and stressed rather the Spirit and the Letter in his interpretation of Scripture. Donne's manipulation of typological biblical images and his application of them to particular and general seventeenth-century themes is much more complicated than that of Milton, for example, and perhaps less traditional than that of Herbert, but it is equally relevant.

[17]   Hughes edition, 35.
[18]   See MacCallum's remarks in this regard, "Milton and the Figurative Interpretation of the Bible", 411.
[19]   Helen C. White, Ruth C. Wallerstein, and Ricardo Quintana, eds., *Seventeenth-Century Verse and Prose,* 2 vols. (New York: The Macmillan Co., 1959), I, 25.
[20]   Ruth C. Wallerstein, *Studies in Seventeenth-Century Poetic,* 212.

Lancelot Andrewes' use of typological reference in his sermons is very similar to that of Donne. In a Christmas Sermon, preached in 1620, Andrewes speaks of:

That which was thus promised to, and by the Patriarchs, shadowed forth in the figures of the Law, the Temple, and the Tabernacle; that which was foresaid by the Prophets, and foresung of in the Psalms, that was this day fulfilled.[21]

And in an earlier Christmas sermon in 1609:

And well also might it be called the fulness of time in another regard. For till then all was but in promise, in shadows and figures and prophecies only, which fill not, God knows. But when the performance of these promises, the body of those shadows, the substance of those figures, the fulfilling or filling full of all those prophecies came, then came 'the fulness of time' truly so called. Till then it came not; then it came.[22]

Typological imagery is prevalent in the poetry as well as in the sermons of the seventeenth century. Helen Gardner speaks of metaphysical poetry and "the twistings of Scripture to yield symbolic meanings, reaching back through the Liturgies and through commentaries on Scripture to the Fathers".[23] Garner points out that "Vaughan's allegorical [typological?] habit of mind ... presupposes history as shadowing forth the providence of God and the immaterial world beyond this".[24] The typological tradition plays a large role in the shaping of Herbert's poetry as well.

This way of interpreting the scriptures was, in the seventeenth century, perfectly orthodox. Professor Tuve has illustrated very fully, in *A Reading of George Herbert*, his use of images derived from the Old Testament which through centuries of employment by the Church, had acquired rich overtones of meaning. Anglicans were still accustomed to associating certain Jewish types with Christian revelations, the Ark pre-figuring the Church, the offering of Isaac, the gift of God's Son, and so forth. Some of Herbert's allusions have become obscure to us, thanks to our neglect both of the Bible and of his habit of drawing analogies; but obvious examples of his fondness for the Old Testament can be seen in *Decay, Sion, Aaron or Affliction V*.[25]

To quote just one or two other examples out of many, the meaning of Jonson's poem on his son takes on a much fuller meaning when it is realized that the poem is written from a typological viewpoint, which

[21] *Nativity Sermons*, 237.
[22] *Nativity Sermons*, 48.
[23] Helen Gardner, *The Metaphysical Poets* (Penguin Books, 1957), 26-27.
[24] Ross Garner, *Henry Vaughan: Experience and the Tradition* (Chicago: University of Chicago Press, 1959), 1.
[25] Margaret Bottrall, *George Herbert* (London: John Murray, 1954), 93.

makes of his son a second Benjamin: "Farewell, thou child of my right hand, and joy ..."[26]

Typology is equally evident in Herrick's "Sabbaths":

> Sabbaths are threefold (as S. Austine says:)
> The first of Time, or Sabbath here of Dayes;
> The second is a Conscience trespasse-free;
> The last the Sabbath of Eternitie.[27]

It is obvious, then, that the typological world view, which is derived from the figurative exegesis of scripture and is based ultimately upon a theology of history that comprehends all events under the eternal relevance of a provident God, is reflected everywhere in the literature of the seventeenth century. It would be literally impossible to trace all the occurrences of typological thinking in the poetry and prose of the period. It is so prevalent that it provides an unwritten and often unexpressed basis for much of the imagery in the literature. Typology was so much taken for granted that it is almost indiscernible to a later age that no longer thinks in the categories of type, antitype and fulfillment.

The second part of the discussion on typology and seventeenth-century literature attempts to trace the manifestations of a typological habit of thought in a few selected typological themes. Seventeenth-century writers still looked upon the Old Testament as finding fulfillment in the New Testament and in contemporary history. Christ was a Second Adam and Mary a Second Eve, as well as a figure of the Church; the continuing redemption wrought by Christ was a New Exodus, and the Flood was a new Creation. Moses, Isaac, Noah and Joshua were meaningful prefigurations of Christ. These examples do not exhaust the possibilities, of course, and there is much room for further investigation into the typological themes of seventeenth-century literature, especially in the application of typological figures and events to contemporary historical events, the "localized expression" of type and antitype in the context of present and contemporary history to which Markus refers.[28] The Chapters that follow pretend to be no more than an introduction to the vast amount of material that awaits further investigation and analysis.

---

[26]   Ben Jonson, *Poems*, ed. George Burke Johnston (London: Routledge and Kegan Paul, Ltd., 1954), 23.

[27]   Robert Herrick, *Poetical Works*, ed. L. C. Martin (Oxford: at the Clarendon Press, 1956), 386.

[28]   Markus, "Presuppositions ...", 76.

VI

THE SECOND ADAM

Not higher that Hill nor wider looking round,
Where on for different cause the Tempter set
Our Second Adam in the Wilderness,
To show him all Earths Kingdoms and thir Glory,
John Milton, *Paradise Lost*, XI, 381-384.

One of the clearest uses of typology in scripture is Paul's reference to Adam as τύπος τοῦ μέλλοντος, a "type of Him who is to come", in Romans 5:14. Paul expands this typological relationship in the 15th Chapter of the First Epistle to the Corinthians, where he speaks of "the First Adam" (ὁ πρῶτος ἄνθρωπος Ἄδαμ) and the "Last Adam" (ὁ ἔσχατος Ἄδαμ).[1] This Christian theme is a common one throughout much of the New Testament and it was taken up and expanded in great detail by the Fathers of the Church.[2] Origen, for example, speaking of Christ, says: "He is not only the first born of all Creation, but is also designated the man, Adam, for Paul says He is Adam: 'The last Adam was made a life-giving Spirit'."[3] The Christ-Adam correspondence is a theme that occurs with great frequency in the literature of the seventeenth century. Donne, for example, at the conclusion of the sermon, *Deaths Duel*, says: "And as God breathed a soul into the first Adam, so this second Adam breathed his soul into God, into the hands of God."[4] The same concept

---

[1] I Cor. 15:22, 44-49. The Greek text in both the Romans and Corinthians passages brings out the typological relationship very clearly.
[2] See Danielou, *From Shadows to Reality*, Book I, Ch. I and III, on Christ and Adam in Scripture and in the Fathers.
[3] *Com. in Joannem.*
[4] John Donne's *Devotions Upon Emergent Occasions* together with *Deaths Duel* (Ann Arbor Paperback: University of Michigan Press, 1959), 189. "... so when he comes to the true Scriptures, and compares the New Testament with the Old, the Gospel with the Law, he finds this to be a performance of those promises, a fulfilling of those Prophecies, a revelation of the Types and figures, and an accomplishment and a possession of those hopes and those reversions ..." — Donne, *Sermons*, ed. Potter and Simpson, I, 298. Also I, 293 for an added Second Adam reference.

is deepened and enlarged with an added typological reference to the
individual soul in Donne's *Hymne to God, my God, in My Sicknesse*:

> We thinke that Paradise and Calvarie,
> Christs Crosse, and Adams tree, stood in one place;
> Looke Lord, and finde both Adams met in me;
> As the first Adams sweat surrounds my face,
> May the last Adams blood my soul embrace.[5]

It is in Milton's three great poems, however, that the typological concept
of the Second Adam is most frequently and clearly expressed. There is a
basic unity which unites the three great poems of Milton's later life, and
this unity is based upon the typological relationship of type and antitype
manifested in *Paradise Lost, Samson Agonistes,* and *Paradise Regained.*
The Christ-Adam correspondence, and the unifying theme connecting
both *Paradise Lost* and *Paradise Regained,* is stated in Book XI of
Paradise Lost:

> Not Higher that hill nor wider looking round,
> Where on for different cause the Tempter set
> Our Second Adam in the wildernesse,
> To show him all earths kingdoms and thir glory.
>   (ll. 381-384)

Milton underlines the general typological structure of his epic in the
opening lines of *Paradise Lost*:

> Of Man's First Disobedience, and the Fruit
> Of that Forbidden Tree, whose mortal taste
> Brought Death into the World, and all our woe,
> With loss of Eden, till one greater Man
> Restore us, and regain the blissful Seat,
> Sing, Heav'nly Muse, that on the secret top
> Of Oreb, or of Sinai, didst inspire
> That Shepherd, who first taught the chosen Seed
> In the Beginning how the Heav'ns and Earth
> Rose out of Chaos ...
>   (ll. 1-10)

Milton here clearly states his theme: the sin of the "First Man, of men
innumerable ordained First Father" (*P.L.* VIII, 297-298) and the
recapitulative restoration of all men in the "Greater Man", who is the
fulfillment of the type expressed in Adam. Man's "first disobedience" is

---

[5]   Donne's *Poetical Works*, ed. Herbert J. Grierson, 2 vols. (Oxford: University Press,
1958), I, 368. All references to the poetry of Donne are from this edition. On this
particular passage, see the note in Helen Gardner, *John Donne: The Divine Poems*
(Oxford: At the Clarendon Press, 1952), 135-137. See also the comments of D. C. Allen,
"John Donne's 'Paradise and Calvarie'", *MLN*, LX (1945).

tu be reversed in the antitype who will "undo" the loss of Eden and all
our woe.[6] This recapitulative and typological action is illumined by
Eternal Providence, and thus, in the context of Divine Relevance and
eternal history, Milton is enabled to "justify the ways of God to man"
(ll. 23-26).

By concentrating in these opening lines references to such widely separated
persons as Adam and Christ, Israel (the "Chosen Seed" descended from
Abraham and an ancestor of Christ who was himself called "the seed of the
woman") and Moses, Milton is appealing to his readers to make a kind of
connection which they were accustomed to make when they read the Bible or
heard it expounded from the pulpit: a vertical or figural connection between
events not horizontally or causally connected except as they were seen as stages
in the history of man's salvation ... Thus in his opening lines Milton is
establishing the atmosphere of the whole poem: an atmosphere in which on
apparent Biblical authority every action, every speech, every description is part
of a great system reaching back into the past of Chaos and the Fall, and
forward into the working out of God's providence in Redemption and
Restoration.[7]

In a similar way, Boman points out, "the story of Adam and Eve embodies the history of mankind".[8] Milton conceived of the Fall, of *Paradise
Lost*, as a type and a figure of a recurring event, repeated in further
types throughout the history of salvation, until it is fulfilled and perfected
in the "one greater Man".[9] Because he takes such a biblical and theological view of history for granted, Milton's typological references are
often implicit, as well as explicitly stated. The battle of the Angels at the
beginning of time is clearly to be understood in the traditional typological framework of the battle of good and evil in the New Testament,
and the battle of the Angels at the end of time as recorded in the Apocalypse 12:4-11. Adam's temptation is only completely 'fulfilled' when it is

[6]   There is an implicit typological reference in the "Chosen Seed" also, for that Seed is
both Israel and Christ (cf. Genesis 3:15, and *P.L.* XII, 379).
[7]   Sims, *The Bible in Milton's Epics*, 11-12. See also Mother Mary Christopher Pecheux,
O.S.U., "The Second Adam and the Church in *Paradise Lost*", *Journal of English
Literary History*, XXXIV (1967), 173-187 and "Abraham, Adam and the Theme of Exile
in *Paradise Lost*", *PMLA*, LXXX (1965), 365-371.
[8]   Boman, *Hebrew Thought Compared With Greek*, 139.
[9]   It is obvious here that I disagree with Ross who feels that Milton represents the
breakdown rather than the culmination of this type of sacramental, typological framework. Ross says: "It is not merely that he ends that tradition" and "In Milton Noah's
Ark cannot be a type of the Church because for Milton the visible Church, if not anti-
Christ, is at the very best, Christless. And significantly, the 'forerunners' of Christ in the
vision vouchsafed to Adam by the Archangel are not Christ types. They are not sacrificed in history but miraculously extricated from it." — M. M. Ross, *Poetry and Dogma*
(New Brunswick, 1954), 183, 99. In such a view, Ross misses the true value of typological relationships which are 'fullfilments' and 'recapitulations' as well as 'repetitions'.

placed side by side with that of *Samson Agonistes* and that of Christ in *Paradise Regained*.

The Second Adam theme actually unites the three great poems of Milton's later life into a harmonious, typological structure. It is obvious that Milton intended *Paradise Regained* to be the end of the story, the fulfillment in the antitype of the type which he had pictured in *Paradise Lost*.

> I who erewhile the happy Garden sung,
> By one man's disobedience lost, now sing
> Recover'd Paradise to all mankind,
> By one man's firm obedience fully tried,
> Through all temptation and the Tempter foil'd
> In all his wiles, defeated and repuls'd,
> And Eden rais'd in the waste wilderness.
>
> (*P.R. I*, 1-7)

Less obvious is the fact that *Samson Agonistes* marks an intermediate stage, a later type, in the fulfillment of the typological correspondence between the Adam of *Paradise Lost* and the Christ of *Paradise Regained*. In discussing the question of why Milton chose to write a poem on Samson, so closely linked with the composition of *Paradise Lost* and *Paradise Regained*, Professor Hanford has suggested that Milton found an analogy between Samson's sin and Adam's.[10] It may be added that there is also an analogy between Samson and Adam. Krouse points out that this Samson-Christ duality was "part of — perhaps even the center of — the meaning which the poet intended the tragedy to have ... this appears to be an inescapable conclusion".[11] To the seventeenth-century reader, steeped in the tradition of Samson as a figurative foreshadowing of Christ, and especially to a reader coming fresh from *Paradise Lost* and *Paradise Regained*, this would have been an inescapable conclusion indeed. It seems obvious then that Milton intended the three great poems to form a typological tryptych.

The basis of this typological unity in the three poems is the recapitulative nature of the Christ-Adam correspondence. The recapitulative nature of typology has been discussed above in Chapter III, especially as this theory was expressed in its broad outlines by St. Paul, and brought to its fullest development in Irenaeus. When Christ became Incarnate:

---

[10] James Holly Hanford, *Studies in Shakespeare, Milton and Donne* (= *University of Michigan Publications in Language and Literature*, I) (New York, 1925).

[11] Michael Krouse, *Milton's Samson and the Christian Tradition* (Princeton: Princeton University Press, 1949), 124.

... he recapitulated in himself the long history of man, summing up and giving us salvation in order that we might receive again in Christ Jesus what we had lost in Adam, that is, the image and likeness of God.[12]

George Herbert expresses the same notion of Christic recapitulation:

> What Adam had, and forfeited for all,
> Christ keepeth now, who cannot fail or fall.[13]

And similarly in Vaughan, the same idea of recapitulative action in Christ, repairing the Fall of Adam, is seen:

> Death, and darkness get you packing,
> Nothing now to man is lacking,
> All your triumphs now are ended,
> And what Adam marr'd, is mended.[14]

Christ's recapitulative action has a twofold aspect. He accomplishes and fulfills what Adam has done, and at the same time, he restores what has been undone by Adam. Christ therefore represents a new creation, a new beginning. In that sense, he is truly a second Adam.

We are concerned with a new beginning (κεφαλή) which is a resumption of the first, while at the same time it both restores the broken harmony (here we have the idea of reparation for sin) and surpasses the original work (the aspect of accomplishment). The Adamic typology has then the special feature of offering at one and the same time difference and similarity.[15]

In Molwitz's definition which has been discussed above, the Adamic typology is accomplished in Christ by the "iteratio Adami ... per idem ac contrarium".[16]

It is this typological recapitulative correspondence between Christ and Adam which unites Milton's *Paradise Lost* and *Paradise Regained* into one harmonious whole. Though the poems represent two successive stages in the history of salvation, they are two parts of one whole. *Paradise Regained* is the completion of the story, the fulfillment and the recapitulation of the account begun in *Paradise Lost*. At the very beginning of *Paradise Regained*, Milton says that what was lost by one man's

[12]   Johannes Quasten, *Patrology* (Westminster, Md.: Newman Press, 1950-1960), I, 296. See also "Christ and Adam in St. Irenaeus", in: Danielou, *From Shadows to Reality*, 30-47.

[13]   "The Holdfast", in: *Works of George Herbert*, ed. F. E. Hutchinson (Oxford: At the Clarendon Press, 1959), 143.

[14]   "Easter Hymn", in: *Vaughan's Works*, ed. L. C. Martin, second edition (Oxford: at the Clarendon Press, 1957), 457. All references to Vaughan and Herbert are to these editions.

[15]   Danielou, *From Shadows to Reality*, 30.

[16]   Cf. p. 45, *supra*.

disobedience is now restored by the obedience of the Second Adam. Milton's prologue is an echo of the Patristic tradition on the Second Adam typology, as expressed, for example by St. Anselm in a classic passage:

It was fitting that as by a man's disobedience death entered the human race, so by a man's obedience should life be restored. And just as sin, which was the cause of our condemnation, had its beginning from a woman, so should the author of our righteousness and salvation be born of a woman. And as the devil had conquered man by tasting of a tree, to which he persuaded him, so by the suffering endured on a tree, which he inflicted, should he, by a man, be conquered.[17]

Milton enuntiates the same unifying theme at the very beginning of *Paradise Lost*, which is practically a paraphrase of the Anselmian typology:

> ... Man's First Disobedience and the Fruit
> Of that Forbidden Tree whose mortal taste
> Brought Death into the World, and all our woe,
> With loss of Eden, till one greater Man
> Restore us, and regain the blissful Seat ...
>   (*P.L.*, I, 1-5)

Through Christ's recapitulative action in *Paradise Regained*, mankind is restored to a state of blessedness. To accomplish this, Christ, the 'second Adam', repeats the experiences of the first Adam, but with the opposite result in each case.

Jesus Christ went over the same ground as Adam, but in the reverse direction. He placed himself in the same circumstances as Adam, and was confronted with the same choices. At every point where Adam weakly yielded, slipping down to destruction, Christ heroically resisted, and at the cost of his agony retrieved the disaster.[18]

"Now thou has avenged supplanted Adam", Milton says, "and by vanguishing Temptation, hast regained lost Paradise."[19]

The Second Adam theme is reflected elsewhere in seventeenth-century

---

[17]   *Cur Deus Homo*? I, 3.
[18]   Lawson, *The Biblical Theology of Saint Irenaeus*, 143-144. "In the typology of the Bible there are two parallel versions of the fall and redemption of man. Adam falls from a garden into a wilderness, losing the tree of life and the water of life; Christ, the second Adam, wins back the Garden ("Eden raised in the waste wildernesse") and restores to man the tree and river of life ... Christ in *Paradise Lost* illustrates the pattern of this positive or real act: all his acts are creative or re-creative (i.e. redemptive). Adam's fall was thus not an act but a failure to act, the sham act of disobedience." N. Frye, "The Typology of *Paradise Regained*", *MP*, LIII (1956), 228, 231.
[19]   *P.R.*, IV, 606-609.

literature. Donne, for example, makes use of the tradition linking Christ's cross and Adam's tree, which is also present in the passage from Anselm:

> We think that Paradise and Calvarie,
> Christs crosse, and Adams tree, stood in one place ...[20]

In *The Sacrifice*, Herbert has Christ express the Adamic relationship:

> So sits the earths great curse in Adams fall
> Upon my head: so I remove it all
> From th'earth unto my brows, and bear the thrall ...[21]

But the Second Adam typology is most evident in Milton, for he alone in the seventeenth century used it not only as a source of poetic imagery, but as the structural basis and unifying principle behind the three great poetic achievements of his life.

Because this typological theme underlying *Paradise Lost* and *Paradise Regained* has been overlooked, there has been a considerable amount of misunderstanding of the last two books of *Paradise Lost* and their relationship to the poem as a whole. Thomas Newton felt that these last two books "fall short of the sublimity and majesty" of the rest of the poem.[22] Lewis maintains that this "untransmuted lump of futurity" spoils the structure of the poem.[23] But actually, just the reverse is true. Far from spoiling the structure of the poem, the vision of the future at the end of *Paradise Lost* actually establishes the basic unity of the poem as just one part of a typological pattern.[24] True enough that these passages may seem extremely dull and meaningless to a modern reader, unused to the typological patterns and traditions of an earlier biblically minded age, but for Milton and his contemporaries, Books XI and XII, with their world wide vision of all history and the story of salvation, represent the climax of *Paradise Lost*, and point the way towards the fulfillment of the typological account of Adam and his Fall in the triumph of Christ over Satan in *Paradise Regained*.

---

[20] See note 5.

[21] George Herbert, *The Sacrifice*, ll, 165-168.

[22] Newton's view is cited in Joseph Summers, *The Muses Method: An Introduction to Paradise Lost* (Cambridge, Mass.: 1962), 186. For other criticisms of these last two books, see also the comments in Summers, 186-187.

[23] C. S. Lewis, *A Preface to Paradise Lost* (London: 1943), 125.

[24] This is substantially the view held by H. R. MacCallum in an article on Milton's view of biblical history in the last two books of *Paradise Lost*. See "Milton and Sacred History: Books XI and XII of *Paradise Lost*", *Essays in English Literature From the Renaissance to the Victorian Age*, ed. Millar MacLure and F. W. Watt (Toronto: University of Toronto Press, 1964), 149-168.

Douglas Bush, on the other hand, indicates the true place of these last two books in the structure of Milton's last three great poems when he says that "... this outline of Hebrew history may be for us rather long and dull" but it is necessary for Milton's structure.[25] The vision of the future is indeed necessary for Milton's structure, because the structure is essentially typological, and *Paradise Lost* thus remains essentially incomplete and unfulfilled. The pattern is incomplete without the necessary fulfillment in the antitype of Christ's victory over Satan and the recapitulative recovery through his own triumph of what Adam had lost through his fall. The type has a value in and of itself but it must be completed at some future time in the plan of salvation. This is the point of the vision presented to Adam at the end of *Paradise Lost*. There is reason for hope, because Adam's fall is not irretrievable. It is to be completed and perfected in the actions of the "one Greater Man" in *Paradise Regained*.

H. R. MacCallum defends the relevance of the last two books of *Paradise Lost* as part of the essential typological structure of the poem as a whole. Milton, he says, is writing in the context of Christian history, following the tradition of Augustine and the Church Fathers who divided the history of the world into six ages. To this concept of Christian history, Milton adds the "theory of Christ's typological presence in the Old Testament".

Since the Old Testament periods ... are typologically related to the New Testament, they will also be related to each other by various correspondences of design. The basic pattern of fall, regeneration and renewal is repeated cyclically from age to age, each new world being born out of the ruins of the old through the man of faith. Yet there is progress, too, a movement from implicit to explicit, "from shadowy Types to Truth, from Flesh to Spirit".

(*P.L.*, XII, 303)[26]

In the typological survey of the history of salvation, MacCallum says that the dominant feature of Milton's typology "is the Pauline and Augustinian emphasis on the men of faith as prefigurations of Christ".[27]

---

[25] Douglas Bush, *Paradise Lost in Our Time* (New York, 1945), 86. There has been a renewed discussion of the place of these last two books in Milton's structure in recent years. See for example: E. M. W. Tillyard's revised view of the crisis in *Paradise Lost* in *Studies in Milton* and F. T. Prince, "On the Last Two Books of *Paradise Lost*", *Essays and Studies*, The English Association, n.s. XI (London, 1958), 38-52. Also Marjorie Nicolson, *John Milton: A Reader's Guide to His Poetry* (New York: Noonday Press, 1963), 315 ff. The most recent discussions of the place of the last two books in Milton's epic are H. R. MacCallum, "Milton and Sacred History", and Louis L. Martz, *The Paradise Within: Studies in Vaughan, Traherne and Milton* (New Haven: Yale University Press, 1964).

[26] MacCallum, "Milton and Sacred History", 153-154.

[27] MacCallum, 158.

Michael's vision of the future represents the whole scope of providential history from Adam to Christ, a history dominated and controlled by the Divine Relevance. Noah, Abraham, Moses, Joshua, David and Solomon are pictured as types of Christ.[28] God's Providence watches over and directs the historical events, gradually bringing them through a slow pedagogy to fulfillment in Christ.

... the prophecy of Michael is also structured so as to display the progressive manifestation of Grace operating throughout human history to create mankind anew by means of Faith.[29]

At the very beginning of the prophecy Michael clearly explains the divine relevance and providence to Adam:

> Adam, thou know'st heav'n his, and all the Earth,
> Not this Rock only; his Omnipresence fills
> Land, Sea and Air ...
> ... surmise not then
> His presence to these narrow bounds confin'd
> Of Paradise of Eden ...
> Yet doubt not but in Valley and in Plain
> God is as here, and will be found alike
> Present, and of his presence many a sign
> Still following thee, still compassing thee round
> With goodness and paternal Love, His face
> Express, and of His steps the track Divine.[30]

The vision of Michael is centered on Christ, the Chosen Seed. The Christic correspondences and the theme of typological fulfillment in Christ keep recurring throughout Book XI and XII, as Michael instructs Adam in the history of the world. At the very beginning of the long dialogue, as they stand upon the hill, "of Paradise the highest" Milton says:

> Not higher that Hill, nor wider looking round,
> Whereon, for different cause the Tempter set

---

[28] Henry F. Robins, *If This Be Heresy* (Urbana: University of Illinois Press, 1963), 173. Sir William Alexander speaks of the patriarchs, kings, and prophets, who "Yet did but Christ by Types and figures see". — *Doomes-day*, 1614, ed. L. E. Kastner and H. B. Charlton (Edinburgh: Scottish Text Society, 1929), n.s. XXIV, 231.

[29] Barbara K. Lewalski, "Structure and Symbolism of Vision in Michael's Prophecy, *PL XI* and *XII*", *PQ*, XLII (1963), 28. Lewalski also says: "This aspect of Michael's prophecy owes something to the widespread tradition of typological exegesis of Old Testament stories ..." — *Ibid*. It is my contention that Michael's prophecy owes more than just a little to typological exegesis, that in fact, the whole of the prophecy is essentially typological, and provides the link between the type and antitype correspondence of *Paradise Lost* and *Paradise Regained*.

[30] *P.L.* XI, 335-355.

> Our Second Adam, in the Wilderness,
> To show him all Earths Kingdoms and thir Glory.
>
> (*P.L.* XI, 381-384)

Immediately, the relationship of Christ and Adam, *Paradise Lost* and *Paradise Regained* is set in a typological context. Noah, "this second source of men"[31] is presented as the antitype of Adam, for Michael tells Adam that in the Flood, he has "seen one world begin and end, and man as from a second stock proceed".[32] At the same time, and in his own right, Noah is the type of the greater Christ who is to come. He is "the only son of light in a dark age" and "one man found so perfect and so just that God vouchsafes to raise another world from him".[33]

The Christological references are especially evident in Book XII. Abraham will be blessed in his seed, and:

> ... By that Seed
> Is meant thy great deliverer, who shall bruise
> The Serpent's head; whereof to thee anon
> Plainlier shall be reveal'd.
>
> (*P.L.* XII, 148-151)

Moses will descend from the mountain of Sinai and will ordain laws for the people:

> ... informing them, by types
> And shadows, of that destin'd Seed to bruise
> The Serpent, by what means he shall achieve
> Mankind's deliverance.
>
> (*P.L.* XII, 232-235)

Michael tells Adam of the Mediator:

> ... whose high Office now
> Moses in figure bears, to introduce
> One greater, of whose day he shall foretell;
> And all the Prophets in thir Age the times
> Of great Messiah shall sing.
>
> (*P.L.* XII, 240-244)

Later in the same passage, Adam asks Michael why there must be so "many and so various laws". Michael replies that they must in time come to a better covenant:

> ... disciplin'd
> From shadowy Types to truth, from Flesh to Spirit,
> From imposition of strict Laws, to free

---

[31] *P.L.*, XII, 13. See also XI, 890.
[32] *P.L.*, XII, 6-7.
[33] *P.L.*, XI, 808-809, 876-877.

> Acceptance of large Grace, from servile fear
> To filial, works of Law to works of Faith.
> (*P.L.* XII, 302-306)

Joshua, "whom the Gentiles Jesus Call", bears the name and office of him,

> ... who shall quell
> The Adversary Serpent, and bring back
> Through the world's wilderness long-wander'd man
> Safe to eternal Paradise of rest.
> (*P.L.* XII, 310-314)

David receives a promise that his throne shall endure forever.

> ... The like shall Sing
> All Prophecy, That of the Royal Stock
> Of David (so I name this King) shall rise
> A Son, the Woman's seed to thee foretold,
> Foretold to Abraham, as in whom shall trust
> All Nations, and to Kings foretold, of Kings
> The last, for of his Reign shall be no end.
> (*P.L.* XII, 324-330)

Antipater succeeds to the throne so "that the true anointed King Messiah might be born barred of his right" (*P.L.* XII, 358-360).

At the end of this chronicle of Old Testament types, Adam says:

> ... now clear I understand
> What oft my steadiest thoughts have searcht in vain,
> Why our great expectation should be call'd
> The Seed of Woman.
> (*P.L.* XII, 376-379)

He asks Michael about the struggle and how the Victor's heel will be bruised. Michael replies that this can be:

> But by fulfilling that which thou didst want,
> Obedience to the Law of God, impos'd
> On penalty of death, and suffering death
> The penalty to thy transgression due ...
> (*P.L.* XII, 396-399)

In Michael's words there is a clear declaration of the recapitulative and typological nature of Christ's triumph as recounted in *Paradise Regained*. As a result of Christ's triumph, the Earth:

> Shall all be Paradise, far happier place
> Than this of Eden, and far happier days.
> (*P.L.* XII, 464-465)

Paradise will be fulfilled and perfected in the final triumph. Michael concludes his vision of the world, summarising the underlying typological structure of all that has been revealed to Adam:

> ... So shall the World go on,
> To good malignant, to bad men benign,
> Under her own weight groaning, till the day
> Appear of respiration to the just
> And vengeance to the wicked, at return
> Of him so lately promis'd to thy aid,
> The Woman's Seed, obscurely then foretold,
> Now amplier known thy Saviour and thy Lord;
> Lost in the Clouds from Heav'n to be revealed
> In glory of the Father, to dissolve
> Satan with his perverted World, then raise
> From the conflagrant mass, purg'd and refin'd,
> New Heav'ns, new Earth, Ages of endless date,
> Founded in righteousness and peace and love,
> To bring forth fruits, Joy and eternal Bliss.[34]

The type is brought to complete fulfillment in the triumph of Christ at the Eschaton. With the hope of this final triumph through the promised Christ, with all the world before them and "Providence their guide"[35] Adam and Eve take the first steps into the history of salvation.

Michael's prophecy is clearly typological, for at every point in his account of the history of salvation, slowly and painfully revealing itself under God's provident hand, there is a reference to Christ who comes as the fulfillment of types and shadows, the antitype completing and bringing to completion the long history of types in the Old Testament. It is thus, that the typological prophecy of Michael at the end of *Paradise Lost* provides the structural link to the fulfillment in *Paradise Regained*.

Commenting on the account of the Temptation of Christ in St. Luke, Ambrose says: "See how the selfsame knots that were tied in condemnation are now undone, and how the old footprints are trodden again in the work of salvation."[36] This is obviously Milton's purpose in *Paradise Lost*. He wishes to present the fulfillment of the type, the recapitulative action of Christ, the Second Adam, who reverses the Fall of the first man

---

[34] *P.L.*, XII, 536-551. In Michael's account of the struggle between Christ and Satan (*P.L.*, XII, 386-465) and in the lines which follow, the Battle of the Angels at the beginning of the epic is used as a type of Christ's battle with Satan and of the final battle of the angels at the end of time, as recorded in the Apocalypse. This same typology is presupposed in *P.R.*, IV, 604-609.

[35] *P.L.*, XII, 646-649.

[36] *Comm. in Lucam*, IV, 7, *PL* 15:1614.

by his own triumph over Satan. The typological theme is clearly expressed at the beginning of *Paradise Regained*, as has been seen above:

> I who erewhile the happy Garden sung,
> By one man's disobedience lost, now sing
> Recover'd Paradise to all mankind,
> By one man's firm obedience fully tried
> Through all temptation and the Tempter foil'd
> In all his wiles, defeated and repulst',
> And Eden rais'd in the waste wilderness.
>
> (*P.R.*, I, 1-7)

The same theme is repeated in God's words to Gabriel:

> He now shall know I can produce a man
> Of female Seed, far abler to resist
> All his solicitations, and at length
> All his vast force, and drive him back to Hell,
> Winning by Conquest what the first man lost
> By fallacy surpris'd ...
>
> ...
>
> His weakness shall o'ercome Satanic strength
> And all the world, and mass of sinful flesh ...
>
> (*P.R.*, I, 150-162)

The recapitulative typological action of Christ in the wilderness is summarized by the Choir of Angels at the conclusion of *Paradise Regained*:

> ... now thou hast aveng'd
> Supplanted Adam, and by vanquishing
> Temptation, hast regain'd lost Paradise,
> And frustrated the conquest fraudulent.
>
> (*P.R.*, IV, 606-609)

Milton is merely echoing the long tradition of Patristic typological interpretation of the temptation of Christ in the Wilderness.[37] In the scriptural story of the temptation, Jesus is put forth as the new Adam, and his temptation by Satan is the sequel, and the fulfillment, of the temptation of Adam. By his victory over Satan in the triple encounter recorded in the Gospels, Christ restores the status which Adam had forfeited by his fall.[38] Christ is the typological fulfillment of Adam, for Christ is the "perfect man"[39] and "the utmost of meer man, both wise

[37] See M. Steiner, *La Tentation de Jésus dans l'interprétation patristique de Saint Justin à Origène*, Études Bibliques (Paris: J. Gabaldi, 1962), and Robert Edward Reiter, "In Adam's Room: A Study of the Adamic Typology of Christ in *Paradise Regained*", *Dissertation Abstracts*, XXV (1964), 3581-3582.

[38] Danielou, *From Shadows to Reality*, 17.

[39] *P.R.*, I, 166.

and good".[40] As Rice points out, in *Paradise Regained*, Milton "... is getting behind the accretions of theological speculation and figuring forth the Christ of the New Testament, the Greater man".[41] Pope makes reference to a picture on the Puerte de las Plasterias of the Cathedral at Santiago where the Fall of Man is balanced not by the Crucifixion, which is the more usual parallel, but by a representation of the temptation of Christ in the desert. She then says:

Long before he [Milton] or the Spanish sculptor were born, the hypothesis that Adam's failure was counterbalanced by the triumph of Christ had become so established and familiar a point of doctrine that the impossibility of tracing the work of poet and sculptor to a common source results simply from the multiplicity and the agreement of the sources available to both.[42]

Satan himself in *Paradise Regained*, equates the temptation of Christ and Adam, and hopes that as he has conquered Adam in the Garden, he may also overcome Christ in the Desert.[43]

The Christ-Adam correspondence in *Paradise Lost* and *Paradise Regained* is based upon Christ's role as Second Adam and Greater Man, who reverses the defeat of the first Adam by Satan. This correspondence is carried out in detail in the actual temptation suffered by Christ at the hands of Satan. In the patristic tradition the two temptations are exactly paralleled, for the temptation to gluttony, vainglory, and avarice to which Adam and Eve succumbed, are the very temptations with which Satan attacks Christ, and which he successfully resists.[44] This tradition is evident in the seventeenth century, and Milton is not the only writer to take advantage of it. Richard Ward, for example, says: "We may

---

[40] *P.R.*, IV, 535-536.

[41] W. G. Rice, "Paradise Regained", *Papers of the Michigan Academy of Sciences, Arts and Letters*, XXII, 496.

[42] Elizabeth M. Pope, *Paradise Regained: The Tradition and the Poem* (New York: Russell and Russell, 1962), 51. The "triple equation" which Pope discusses in Chapter V, 51ff. of her volume, is actually a typological relationship, although she does not use the terminology. In fact, much of her volume bears witness to the typological structure of *Paradise Regained*, although she does not seem to be aware of the implications of the concept in Milton. Similarly Northrop Frye, "The Typology of *Paradise Regained*", 227-238. Frye's title is rather deceptive, for although he does maintain that *Paradise Regained* represents the antitype of the Fall of Adam, there is very little actual typology. The article is rather an analysis of the temptations of *Paradise Regained*.

[43] *P.R.*, I, 100-105; II, 132-143.

[44] See the patristic references in Pope, 52. In addition to the similarity of the Temptations, the Fathers have seen an added correspondence between Christ and Adam in the fact that neither was disturbed by the beasts in the Garden or in the Desert. See Pope, 108-110, for references to this tradition in other seventeenth-century writers, Cradock, Giles Fletcher, T. Taylor and others. She says: "... Christ like Adam, went unmolested by the beasts, because like Adam, he was perfect man ..." (109).

observe how he [Satan] begins with the Second Adam, as he did with the first, at the Belly."[45] John Lightfoot makes the typological link between the temptations of Adam and Christ very explicitly:

As our Mother Eve was tempted by Satan to the "lust of the flesh, the lust of the eyes, and the pride of life" (for she saw that it was good for food, that it was pleasant to the eyes, and to be desired to make one wise) so by these, had it been possible, would the tempter have overthrown the seed of the woman: for he tempted him to turn stones into bread, so as to satisfy the longing of the flesh; to fall down and worship him upon the sight of a bewitching object to his eyes; and to fly through the air in pride, and to get glory among men.[46]

Lancelot Andrewes makes use of the same tradition in one of his sermons, which indicates the prevalence of the tradition even in the common mind. It is a passage that is very similar to that of Lightfoot:

... as it is true that Paul saith, that Christ resembled Adam, and was made a "quickening spirit", as a "living soul", ... so may Christ and Adam be compared in these three temptations. For they are both tempted with "concupiscence of the flesh, concupiscence of the eye, and pride of life". In Adam the devil first brought him to a conceit that God envied his good, and of purpose kept him hoodwinked lest he should see his good, as we see falconers put hoods over hawks' eyes, to make them more quiet and ruly. Secondly, he lulls him on to a proud conceit of himself, by persuading him that by eating he should be like God. Thirdly, he showeth the fruit, which was pleasant. So in Christ's temptation: first, he would have brought him to murmur against God; secondly to presume; and thirdly, to commit idolatry ... and under these heads come all temptations.[47]

The framework of Andrewes' sermon is clearly typological, and the crux of the comparison is the similarity in the temptations, though Christ overcomes, and thus fulfills, as *forma perfectior* of the type, the shadow and the figure in the Garden. This is the tradition which was familiar to Milton and which he used to such good advantage in *Paradise Regained*.

Samson Agonistes represents an intermediate step in the progression of salvation history from type to antitype, from Adam to Christ, from *Paradise Lost* to *Paradise Regained*. In Milton's overall conception of the typological unity of his three great poems, Samson is the antitype of

[45] Richard Ward, *Theological Questions, dogmaticall observations, and evangelicall essays, upon the Gospel of Jesus Christ, according to St. Matthew* (London, 1640).
[46] John Lightfoot, *A Harmony of the Gospels*, 1654, reprinted in *Works*, ed. John Rogers Pitman, 13 volumes (London, 1822-1825), III, 42. Note that in these references, the Sins of Adam and Eve are often treated as one, and Christ actually recapitulates the sin of Adam-Eve.
[47] Lancelot Andrewes, *Ninety-Six Sermons*, ed. John Parkinson (Oxford, 1841-1843), 496-497.

Adam, a second, though still inferior Adam, and at the same time a type of Christ whose triumph will be perfect in every way. Though by no means necessary, it would be interesting if it could be shown that Milton composed *Samson Agonistes* after *Paradise Lost* and before he had begun work on *Paradise Regained*, thus paralleling in his own composition the growth of the typological theme to perfection in Christ through Samson.[48]

The basis for the Samson typology is in Hebrews 11:32-40 where Samson is listed with Gedeon, Barac, Jephte, David, Samuel and the prophets whose faith subdued kingdoms. "One and all gave proof of their faith, yet they never saw the promise fulfilled." Milton has taken just one example from the long history of types which he has outlined in Michael's vision at the end of *Paradise Lost*, and told the story in detail, using it as a link in the Christ-Adam typological structure of the two great poems on Paradise.

The Samson-Christ typology is a standard theme in the Patristic tradition, and the same theme was used by the Scholastics as well.[49] Isidore, for example, says Samson: "... habet quiddam in typo gestum Christi".[50] Aelfric comments that: "Samson betokened our Saviour, who by his own death overcame the Devil, triumphed over Satan's power, and redeemed mankind."[51] The Middle Ages concentrated on the correspondence between Samson and *Christus Victor*, and described the desert temptation and the temptation of Samson as a struggle between rival adversaries or athletes.[52] This is the basis of Milton's conception of Samson as Agonistes. Christ is a Victor "... who came off triumphantly from his encounter with Satan in the wilderness".[53]

The tradition of Samson as a type of Christ was still very prevalent in the seventeenth century and it is impossible to suppose that Milton would not have been aware of the deeper theological implications of the story of Samson. Cornelius a Lapide in 1664 clearly examines the typological

---

[48]   See the discussion of the date of *S.A.* in the Hughes' edition, 537-542.
[49]   See for example, the references in Krouse, *Milton's Samson and the Christian Tradition*.
[50]   *PL*, 83:389 ff. See also Bede, *Quaest. Super Librum Judicum*, VII, *PL*, 93:428 ff.; Augustine, *Sermo de Samsone, Sermo*, 364, *PL*, 39:1642 ff.; Ambrose, *PL*, 16:1027 ff. and *PL*, 17:854; Hugh of St. Victor, *PL* 95:680.
[51]   Cited by Krouse, 50.
[52]   Pope, *Paradise Regained: The Tradition and the Poem*, 115 ff.
[53]   Krouse, *Milton's Samson and the Christian Tradition*, 113. See also Clement of Alexandria, *Exhortation* X: "Fashioning himself in flesh he enacted the drama of human salvation: for he was a true champion and a fellow champion with the creature." Scott-Craig says: "Samson Agonistes is really Christus Agonistes", and he maintains that *S.A.* is really a type of Christ's Agony in the Garden. T.S.K. Scott-Craig, "Concerning Milton's *Samson*", *Renaissance News*, V (1952), 43-53.

implications of the Samson-Christ relationship.[54] Krouse reprints a
table from Thomas Haynes, "Wherein Sampson Resembled Christ",[55]
and George Herbert uses the typological similarity in his poem *Sunday*:

> The rest of our Creation
> Our great Redeemer did remove
> With the same shake, which at his passion
> Did th' earth and all things with it move,
> As Samson bore the doors away,
> Christs hands, though nail'd wrought our salvation,
> And did unhinge that day.[56]

Krouse then continues:

There can be no doubt that the allegorical [typological?] interpretation of
Samson as a figure of Christ was, in the seventeenth century, one of the most
prevalent connotations of the hero of Milton's tragedy. It is impossible to
suppose that any of Milton's literate contemporaries could have thought of
Samson without thinking also of Christ.[57]

Further on, Krouse summarizes the basic unity which connects *Paradise
Lost* with *Paradise Regained* through *Samson Agonistes* as the intermediary typological link:

Samson stands for more than the victorious Nazarite, the faithful champion of
God. He brings to full circle the immense story which Milton took up in
Paradise Lost and continued in *Paradise Regained*. In Eden man was tempted,
succumbed to temptation and fell from grace. In the wilderness Christ, in the
role of Redeemer, atoned for Man's sin and restored him to grace by winning
against Satan the victory which alone makes all victory possible. But *Paradise
Regained* did not complete the cycle. There Christ took on the flesh and
appeared as the Son of God, an aspect of the divine. It was left to demonstrate
the victory on the human level. Samson's story, paralleling as it does the story
of *Christus Victor*, reveals him as *Homo Victor*, a palpable exemplification of
the meaning to Man of his Redemption.[58]

Krouse here indicates the integral unity of the three great poems, but
misses the deeper implications of the typological structure, and thus
misplaces Samson in the progress of the story of Salvation. For Samson
is not the completion of the cycle; he is rather an intermediary type, still
only a shadow of Him who is to come.

[54] *Commentarius in Joshue, Judicum et Ruth* (Antwerp, 1664), 175.
[55] Thomas Haynes, *The General View of Holy Scripture* (London, 1640), 217-218.
The table is reproduced as Illustration III and IV in Krouse, 69.
[56] George Herbert, *Works*, 76.
[57] Krouse, 120. See also pp. 119-124, and Madsen, *From Shadowy Types to Truth*,
181-202. But note the disagreement of the critics cited in Hughes' Introduction to
S.A., 541.
[58] Krouse, *Milton's Samson and the Christian Tradition*, 132-133.

Samson's action is semi-recapitulative, therefore; it lacks the perfection and fulfillment of the recapitulative typological action of Christ. Samson is, as Ross says, a "half-Christ".[59] He is not fully Christ, nor indeed, can he be, for he represents just one further step, one deeper fulfillment of the progress that leads to Christ, the *forma perfectior*. This is very clear in Milton's treatment of the temptations of Samson. There is a basic similarity in the temptations of Adam, Samson, and Christ.[60] But Adam has yielded and fallen; Samson has yielded, but then recovers, and overcomes Satan to bring about eventual triumph. Christ, suffering the same three basic temptations as both Adam and Samson, does not yield or waver at all. His triumph is complete. He is the perfected Antitype.

---

[59] M. M. Ross, *Poetry and Dogma*, 223. Ross uses the phrase "half-Christ" in a different context, for, also misunderstanding the deeper typological implications, he maintains that Samson is not a type of Christ. See pp. 12-13.

[60] See Hughes edition, 540 ff.

VII

EVE AND THE GARDEN

> May we have leave
> To think old Eve
> No more unhappy, who have found
> The cure, and may
> With Triumph say
> Eve's Gall in Marie's Sweets are dround.
> Joseph Beaumont, Haile Full of Grace.

One of the essential points of correspondence between Adam and Christ in the Second Adam typology, is the relationship of each to a woman. Adam sinned and fell through a woman, and Christ conquers and triumphs, likewise through a woman. This correspondence actually forms the basis for a separate but related typological theme in the exegesis of the Fathers — the theme of the Second Eve. Irenaeus says:

... when this man was to be restored to grace, God wished the same path to be followed and Christ to be born in the flesh of the virgin by God's will and wisdom; and as the first man fell into sin and death through a virgin's disobedience, so mankind was to find life for his soul through a virgin who was obedient to the word of God.[1]

The Fathers found many points of typical relationship between Christ and Adam, and Eve and Mary. Both Adam and Christ were born of a virgin; Adam from the Virgin earth and Christ from the Virgin Mary. The disobedience of Eve led to Adam's Fall; the obedience of Mary led to Christ's triumph, as Irenaeus recounts in the passage quoted above.[2]

Mary thus represents a secondary recapitulative action with relation to Eve. She sums up, perfects, and reverses the action of Eve in the Garden. By her own actions, she retraces the steps of Eve, but in the opposite direction.

See how the selfsame knots that were tied in condemnation are now undone, and how the old footprints are trodden again in the work of salvation. Adam

---

[1] *Epideixas*, I, 32-33. See also *Adv. Haer.*, IV, 33, 4, *PG* 7:1074.
[2] See also Irenaeus, *Adv. Haer.*, III, 21, *PG* 7:955 and Justin, *Dialog.*, L., 45.

was from the virgin earth, Christ from a Virgin; folly came from a woman, wisdom from a virgin; from the tree came death, from the cross came life.[3]

Epiphanius of Salamis expresses the typological correspondence between Eve and Mary:

Eve looks forward to Mary, and her very name, "Mother of all the living" (Gen. 3:20) is a mysterious presage of the future, for Life itself was born of Mary, whence she became *more fully* "Mother of all the living" ... Nor can we see the passage "I will put enmities between thee and the woman" (Gen. 3:15) as applying to Eve alone; it received its *true fulfillment* when that holy and unique one came, born of Mary, without work of man ...[4]

In the long history of biblical exegesis, the Fathers found many points of correspondence between the First Eve and the Second Eve. Both Eve and Mary were Virgins in the moment of typological crisis, Mary remaining "ever virgin". Eve is visited by the Fallen Angel and tempted; Mary is visited by a good Angel with news of the coming of the Second Adam through her womb. Eve disobeys, while Mary obeys the word of God, and thus Eve brings forth death and Mary brings forth Life. Eve's temptation scene in the Garden is paralleled by Mary's Annunciation. In each case there is a correspondence between Mary and Eve, but also a fulfillment, a *forma perfectior*. The events, one at the beginning of the Old Testament and the other at the beginning of the New Covenant, are clearly typological. The Christic correspondence is expressed in the link provided by the prophecy of the Seed of the Woman in Genesis 3:15. God's Providence is manifest in both events, controlling the progress of salvific history through the two Eves.[5]

Joseph Beaumont's *Haile Full of Grace* is one example of this Second Eve typological theme in the literature of the seventeenth century:

> May we have place
> To heap our prayers on thy crowne,
> About whose wreathe
> All sweets doe breathe
> And Heav'ns illustrious Joyes are throwne.

---

[3]   Ambrose, *Comm. in Lucam*, IV, 7, *PL* 15:1614.

[4]   *Panarion*, III, 2, 78, *PG* 42:728-729. The added emphasis is mine. Justine Martyr was one of the earliest to introduce the idea of the Second Eve. See *Dial. Tryph.*, III.

[5]   For other Patristic references, see for example, Ambrose, *Exposit, in Lucam*, II, 28, *PL* 15:1643; Jerome, *Epistola*, XXII, 21, *PL* 22:408; Irenaeus, *Adv. Haer.*, III, 32, 4, *PG* 7:958-959 and *Adv. Haer.*, V, 19, 1, *PG* 7:1175-1176; Tertullian, *De Carne Christi*, XVII, *PL* 2:827-828; John Damascene, Hom. 2 in *Nat. B. Mariae Virginis*, 5, *PG* 96:687. For additional patristic references see Mother Mary Christopher Pecheux, O.S.U., "The Concept of the Second Eve in Paradise Lost", *PMLA*, LXXV (1960), 359-366.

May we have leave
To think old Eve
No more unhappy, who have found
The Cure, and may
With triumph say
Eve's Gall in Marie's Sweets are dround.[6]

Crashaw's *Hymn on the Assumption of the Blessed Virgin*[7] is another example of the Second Eve typology, and indicates the basic notes of the Eve and Mary correspondence. Eve's sin brought death and the grave; Mary brought life and new Heaven, returning all the stars which Eve stole away:

The First Eve, mother of our Fall,
E'er she bore anyone, slew all.
Of her unkind gift might we have
The inheritance of a hasty Grave;
Quick burye'd in the wanton Tomb
Of one forbidden bitt;
Had not a Better Fruit forbidden it,
Had not thy healthful Womb
The world's new eastern window bin
And given us Heav'n again, in giving Him.
Thine was the Rosy Dawn that sprung the Day
Which renders all the starres she stole away.
(ll. 11-22)

Mary's recapitulative action repairs the fall of Eve and therefore:

'Tis gratitude to forget that other
And call the Maiden Eve their mother.
(ll. 25-26)

Eve's disobedience, "the one forbidden bitt", had shut the door and sealed the fountain of life, but Mary's Virgin womb, sealed and shut, let in Life:

---

[6] Joseph Beaumont, *The Minor Poems*, ed. E. Robinson (New York, 1914), 170.
[7] "The Himn *O Gloriose Domine*", in: *The Poems of Richard Crashaw*, ed. L. C. Martin (Oxford: at the Clarendon Press, 1957), 302-303. Crashaw's poem is a free paraphrase of the hymn from the Roman Breviary. The Latin text is as follows:

O gloriosa virginum,   Tu Regis alti janua
Sublimis inter sidera,   Et aula lucis fulgida:
Qui te creavit, parvulum   Vitam datam per Virginem,
Lactente nutris ubere.   Gentes redemptae, plaudite.

Quod Heva tristis abstulit,   Jesu tibi sit gloria
Tu reddis almo germine   Qui natus est de Virgine,
Intrent ut astra flebiles,   Cum Patre et almo Spiritu,
Caeli recludis cardines.   In sempiterna saecula.
                                              Amen.

Let hearts and lips speak lowd; and say
Hail, door of life! and sourse of day!
The door was shutt, the fountain seal'd;
Yet light was seen and Life revealed.
The door was shutt, yet let in day,
The fountain seald, yet life found way.

(ll. 31-36)

As might be expected, it is John Milton who makes the greatest use of
the Second Eve in *Paradise Lost*, because of the theme's close connection
with the Second Adam typology which is at the basis of Milton's three
great poems. There are two explicit references to the Second Eve in
Paradise Lost. In Book V, Milton says:

... On whom the Angel Hail
Bestow'd, the holy salutation us'd
Long after to blest Mary, second Eve.

(*P.L.*, V, 385-387)

And again towards the end of the epic:

Between Thee and the Woman I will put
Enmity, and between thine and her Seed;
Her Seed shall bruise thy head, thou bruise his heel.
      So spoke this Oracle, then verifi'd
When Jesus son of Mary second Eve,
Saw Satan fall like Lightning down from Heav'n
Prince of the Air ...

(*P.L.*, X, 179-185)

The passage summarizes the Second Eve typology, in the tradition of the
Fathers, as interpreted by Milton in his typological tryptych — *Paradise
Lost, Paradise Regained*, and *Samson Agonistes*. The essential correspondence between type and antitype in the Seed of the Woman is
clearly indicated, as well as the struggle with Satan.

Milton's use of the Second Eve typology and its constituent elements
has been admirably discussed by Mother Pecheux in an article on "The
Concept of the Second Eve in *Paradise Lost*".[8] She examines "the connotations of the concept of the Second Eve as they were elaborated in
some of the Church Fathers with whom Milton was familiar" and attempts "to see how he exploited those connotations to give added
richness to his epic".[9] Milton refers to two passages by Irenaeus on the
Second Eve analogy in *Of Prelaticall Episcopacy*.[10]

[8]   *Loc. cit.*
[9]   Mother Pecheux, 359.
[10] *The Works of John Milton*, Columbia Edition, ed. Frank A. Patterson, 18 volumes
(New York, 1931-1940), III, 94.

Milton's direct reference to the two passages in Irenaeus is proof that he knew at least one patristic statement on the Second Eve; his general knowledge of the Church Fathers suggests that he probably knew others as well. No doubt he was familiar with the Renaissance statements of the doctrine. Certainty on his own immediate sources is less important for an appreciation of its use in the poem than an awareness of the tradition ...[11]

The recurrent motif of the "Seed of the Woman" in Michael's vision in Books XI and XII of *Paradise Lost* illustrates the close connection of the Second Eve and Second Adam types in Milton's thought. Much of what has been said above in the analysis of those last two books of *Paradise Lost* has equal application for the Second Eve typological theme in Milton. Mother Pecheux concludes:

Characteristically, Milton works with great freedom in adapting the tradition he finds; when he takes over the Eve-Mary parallel he boldly modifies the concept of virginity in Eve; he emphasizes the analogies more in other parts of the poem than in the temptation scene; and throughout even the last books, it is less, perhaps, that Eve is absorbed in Mary than that Mary is absorbed in Eve.[12]

She comments on the profoundly Christian optimism of the poem,[13] and this is certainly manifest, and a direct corollary from Milton's use of typological themes as the basic structure of his great biblical poems. For the typological structure with its completion and perfection in Christ must be essentially optimistic.[14]

In the patristic tradition, the Second Adam and Second Eve types are further related by the tradition which saw Eve as a type of the Church, and the sleep of Adam which gave birth to Eve, an image of the death of Christ which gave birth to the Church. Augustine expresses this typology:

[11] Pecheux, 359, note.
[12] Pecheux, 366.
[13] *Ibid.*
[14] A variant on the Eve-Mary typological theme is the Eve-Magdalen relationship. The tradition is not as prominent as the Eve-Mary analogy in the Fathers, but there are numerous references to Eve as a figure of Mary Magdalen. See, for example, Hippolytus, in *Comm. in Cant.*; Gregory of Nyssa, *Contra Eunon.*, XII, *PG* 45:892; Ambrose, *De Isaac*, V, 43 and *Exp. in Lucam*, X, 156. The Eve-Mary typology is *per contrarium*, and the Eve-Magdalen relationship is *per idem*. Magdalen would represent a half-way stage in the progressive development of the Eve-Mary typology, similar to the role of Samson in the Adam-Christ analogy as interpreted by Milton. Magdalen sinned, as did Eve, but she also comes to fuller life and forgiveness at the feet of Christ, thus approaching the role of Mary. Milton may be using an implicit typological relationship between Eve and Magdalen in *P.L.*, V, 129ff. and X, 910 ff. where the descriptions of Eve's tears and hair bear a close relation to the Magdalen story in Luke 7:37ff.

Eve was born from the side of her sleeping spouse, and the Church was born from the dead Christ by the mystery of blood which gushed forth from his side.[15]

The relationship of the three typological themes — Christ and Adam, Eve and Mary, and Eve and the Church — is seen very clearly in the following passage from Augustine:

These words [of Genesis] are a great mystery; here is the symbol pointing forward to the Church that is to come: she is fashioned out of the side of her spouse, out of the side of her spouse in the sleep of death. Did not the Apostle say of Adam that he is "a figure of him who was to come" (Rom. 5:14)? And is it not also true of the Church? Listen, then, understand and realize: it is she that will tread down the serpent's head.[16]

Because of the Eve-Mary analogy, it was a logical development from the concept of Eve as a type of the Church to the further figure of Mary as a type of the Church. Christ is the Second Adam, and the Church born from Christ's side is typified by Mary, the Second Eve. Epiphanius of Salamis weaves these typological strands together into one harmonious figure:

And then there is that other text nearby, "Wherefore a man shall leave father and mother and he shall cleave to his wife, and they shall be two in one flesh" (Gen. 2:24), and this also we can understand of Mary, and I would even say of the Church, for the Apostle says of this passage, "This is a great mystery — I mean in reference to Christ and the Church" (Eph. 3:32). His own body he fashioned from Mary, and the Church he fashioned from the wound in his side, when the spear pierced his breast and there flowed out for us the twin redeeming mysteries of the water and the blood.[17]

The early Church and the patristic tradition saw Mary and the Church as a single figure, "type and antitype from one print as soul and wax".[18]

---

[15] *Contra Faust.*, XII, 8, *PL* 42:258. Tertullian says similarly: "If in truth Adam gave a figure concerning Christ, the sleep of Adam was that death of Christ which he should sleep to death, that from the injury to his side the true mother of all living things, the Church, should be figured." — *De Anima*, Ch. 17. See also Ambrose, *Expos. in Lucam* II, 85-89, *PL* 15:1666-1668; and Hilary, *Tract. Mysteriorum*, I, 1. For a summary on the patristic tradition of the Sleep of Adam, see Danielou, *From Shadows to Reality*, Ch. IV.

[16] *Enarr. In Psalmos*, 103, 6, *PL* 37:1381.

[17] *Panarion* III, 2, 78, *PG* 42:728-729.

[18] H. Rahner, *Our Lady and the Church*, tr. Sebastian Bullough, O.P. (New York: Pantheon Books, 1961), 7. Similarly, Otto Semmelroth, *Urbild der Kirche* (Wurzburg, 1950), 36. For representative patristic citations see Cyril of Alexandria, *Homiliae Diversae*, *PG* 77:996 and Ambrose, *Expos in Lucam*, 2, 7. The Mary-Church relationship is a very rich one in the exegetical literature. See, for example, in addition to the references above, J. B. Terrien, "Parallèle entre Marie et l'Église", *La Mère de Dieu et la Mère des hommes d'après les Pères et la Theologie* (Paris, 1902), II, 1-27; S. Tromp,

One of the basic elements of the theology of the Church found at the beginning in the Apocalypse of John, and then through the early fathers, Justin, Irenaeus and Hippolytus, onwards through Augustine to the *Summa* of Aquinas, is the idea of the Church as the "Mother of the living". This idea is linked with that of Eve, as the first mother of the living and in turn receives fulfillment in Mary giving birth to the living God. Eve, Mary, and the Church: for the early theologians these three formed but one picture with three transparencies. Mary owes her position as the Second Eve and Mother of God's new human race to her dignity as Mother of God: and similarly the Church owes her position to the fact of her being the mother of the Mystical Body of Christ, the mediatrix of divine life and virgin mother of all men whose life is in Christ ... In patristic thought Mary is the *typos* of the Church: symbol, central idea, and as it were, summary of all that is meant by the Church in her nature and vocation.[19]

The Mary-Church typology, with its background of Eve-Church analogy, is based on a triple correspondence existing between the two terms of the typological relationship. Both Mary and Church (and also Eve in her own right) are Mother, Virgin, and Spouse. Mary is the Mother of Christ and Mother of Man; the Church is Mother of all men. As Augustine says:

As Mary gave birth to him who is your head, so the Church gives birth to you. For the Church also is both Mother and Virgin: mother in the womb of love, virgin in her inviolate faith. She is the mother of many nations who are yet one body and are thus likened to that one Virgin Mary, the mother of many but yet of the one.[20]

As Augustine points out, both Mary and the Church are also virgin, and Isaac de Stella expands this notion:

Each of the two is mother, each of the two is Virgin. Each conceives by the same spirit without carnal attraction, each without sin brings forth an offspring to God the Father. Mary without sin provides the head for the body: the church by the remission of sins provides the body for the head. Each is the mother of Christ, but neither gives birth to the whole without the other. Therefore, in the divinely inspired Scripture, what is said individually of Mary; and what is said in a special way of Mary, virgin and mother, is understood by right, but in a general way, of the Church, virgin and mother; so that, when the scripture is understood to be speaking of either, it can be applied to one or the other almost indifferently and in a mixed manner.[21]

"Ecclesia Sponsa Virgo Mater", *Gregorianum* XVIII (1937), 3-29; Y. Congar, "Marie et l'Église dans la pensée patristique", *Revue des Sciences Philosophiques et Théologiques*, XXXVIII (1954), 3-38 and *Christ, Our Lady and the Church* (Westminster: Newman, 1957); Karl Rahner, *Mary, Mother of the Lord* (New York, 1963); E. Schillebeekx, *Marie, Mère de la Redemption* (Paris, 1963); and Walter J. Burghardt, S.J., "Theotokos: The Mother of God", in: *The Mystery of the Woman*, ed. Edward D. O'Connor, C.S.C. (Notre Dame, Ind.: University of Notre Dame Press, 1956).

[19] H. Rahner, *Our Lady and the Church*, 4-5.
[20] *Sermo 25, 8, PL* 38:1013. See also *Sermo* 195, 2.
[21] *Sermon 61 on Assumption, PL* 194:1863, 1865.

Isaac goes on to indicate that just as Mary is the spouse of God, the Church is the spouse of Christ.

It is this third element, the notion of the spouse, which is most common in the literature of the seventeenth century. The references to the Church as the spouse of Christ are frequent in the polemical writings. Milton, for example, calls Christ the "Church's husband" in *The Reason of Church Government*,[22] and Vaughan begins his poem, *The Knot*, with a reference to Mary as spouse of God.

> Bright Queen of Heaven! Gods Virgin Spouse
> The Glad worlds blessed maid!
> Whose beauty tyed life to thy house,
> And brought us saving ayd.
>   (ll. 1-4)

The same reference occurs at the conclusion of Vaughan's *The World*:

> But as I did their madness so discusse
> One whisper'd thus,
> This Ring the Bridegroome did for none provide
> But for his bride.
>   (ll. 56-60)

Donne makes full use of the marriage typology in a sermon preached at the marriage of Mistress Margaret Washington on May 30, 1621:

The first marriage that was made, God made, and he made it in Paradise ... The last marriage which shall be made, God shall make too, and in Paradise too; in the Kingdome of heaven: and at that marriage, I hope in him that shall make it, to meet not some, but all this company. The marriage in this text (Hosea 2:19) hath relation to both those marriages: It is itself the spirituall and mysticall marriage of Christ Jesus to the Church, and to every marriageable soule in the Church. And it hath a retrospect, it looks back to the first marriage ... And then it hath a prospect to the last marriage. ...[23]

Donne's controversial sonnet on the Church begins with the same theme: "Showe me, deare Christ, thy spouse, so bright and cleare".[24] Gardner indicates the source of the imagery of the sonnet in the typological bride of the Apocalypse,[25] and then continues:

The sonnet opens with a prayer to Christ to reveal his Bride to man's sight. This is followed by an expression of incredulity as Donne looks out upon the world of his day and sees how unbridelike are those who claim to be the Spouse

---

[22] Hughes edition, 644.
[23] Gill, *Sacred Philosophy of Holy Scripture*, 68 and *passim*.
[24] Gardner, *Divine Poems*, 15. Compare Satyre III on the same subject.
[25] Gardner, 121-122.

of Christ ... the image in the sonnet is not merely lack of comeliness, but of spoilation, even of loss of virginity.[26]

The typological references, except in the opening line, are not explicit, but the whole framework of the poem, and the basis of the imagery depends upon the assumption of the whole context of the Mary-Eve-Church figure.

The Canticle of Solomon has provided the richest store of images for the Mary-Church relationship, and the Church as the spouse of Christ. In his explanation of the Canticle, Denis the Carthusian systematically applies each chapter of the Canticle in sequence to Mary, to the Church, and to the individual soul.[27] Crashaw's poem on the Assumption of the Blessed Virgin clearly equates Mary with the beloved of the Canticle:

> Rise up, my fair, my spottlesse one!
> The winter's past, the rain is gone.
> The spring is come, the flowers appear.
> No sweets but thou are wanting here.[28]

Application of typological themes to seventeenth-century literature, or to any body of literature for that matter, is a precarious occupation. Since the literary images are already one step removed from the biblical text, the danger is ever present that the concept of strict typology may become so broad as to include what is actually allegory. The danger is correspondingly increased when literary themes and images are discussed, for there is the added temptation to elevate mere biblical allusions to the level of strict typological references. Danielou has discussed this problem in his chapter on the Paradise of the Virtues, where he carefully distinguishes Philonian allegory on the Garden of Paradise and genuine typology.[29] This is especially true in discussing the themes of Paradise, Innocence and the Fall in seventeenth-century literature.

Yet, although seventeenth-century references to the Garden may be colored by overtones of allegory, and in some cases may be nothing more than allegory, there are many cases of fairly strict typological reference to the Garden. The basic framework of this typology is the relationship of the Garden of Eden before the Fall, the state of man's original innocence, and the New Paradise, the New Jerusalem at the end of time, the Paradise of Heaven. The typological link between these two states is seen in the Apocalypse, especially in Chapters 20-22, where the

[26]   Gardner, 122-123.
[27]   *Enarratio in Canticum Canticorum Solomonis, Opera Omnia* (Monstrolii, 1898), VII, 289-447.
[28]   *The Poems*, p. 304, ll. 9-12.
[29]   Danielou, *From Shadows to Reality*, Ch. V, 57 ff.

allusions to the triumph over the serpent, the Church as the New Eve, the river of life and the tree of life, form the basis of the correspondence. Milton is witness to an added typological reference, when he speaks of the "Paradise Within", the state of innocence and goodness in the soul of the individual.[30]

In literary works, and this is also true of the seventeenth century, the concept of Paradise came to be equated with the pagan myth of the Golden Age. But in strict typological terms this must be a *New* Golden Age, which is the fulfillment and perfection of the Old Paradise. As Goppelt points out, it is not a question of a *Wiederkehr*, a return to the Old Age, but of a new and essentially perfected and fulfilled Paradise.[31]

There can be no doubt that the golden age of the classics was frequently identified with this happy, though brief time before the fall. It was commonplace for the commentators to quote Ovid, Lucan and the other classical poets who wrote of the golden age, and some of the commentators add that the heathen poets knew of the state of innocence either from Moses or from a faint memory which yet remained of that happiest time, though of course they debased the true account with fable.[32]

This theme of Paradise is a common one in seventeenth-century literature, either as a retrospective nostalgia for the old Golden Age, or as a true typological foreshadowing of the New Jerusalem and the New Paradise. Milton says in the *Nativity Ode* that with the fulfillment in the Birth of Christ:

> Time will run back, and fetch the age of gold,
> And speckl'd vanity
> Will sicken soon and die,
> And leprous sin will melt from earthly mold,
> And hell itself will pass away,
> And leave her dolorous mansion to the peering day.
>
> (ll. 135-140)

There is more than a simple return of the Old Age of Gold; it represents a fulfillment and a completion, "And Heav'n as at some festival, will open wide the gates of Her high Palace Hall" (ll. 147-148). Christ's triumph over the pagan Gods is an essential element in Milton's conception of the new Age of Gold. In terms reminiscent of the patristic explanations of typology, Joseph Mead says that "those false lights of the Heathen" must

---

[30] *P.L.*, XII, 587.
[31] Goppelt, *Typos: Die Typologische Deutung des alten Testaments im Neuen*, 158.
[32] Arnold Williams, *The Common Expositor*, 108. Cf. pp. 94-138 for a summary of the tradition of Paradise and the State of Innocence and the Fall in the Renaissance.

"vanish when the Sun of righteousness, Christ Jesus, arose into the world".[33]

In *Twicknam Garden,* Donne uses the Paradise imagery:

> But O, selfe traitor, I do bring
> The spider love, which transubstantiates all,
> And can convert Manna to Gall,
> And that this place may thoroughly be thought
> True Paradise, I have the serpent brought.
>
> (ll. 5-9)

In more optimistic mood, Vaughan employs the same image in his poem, *Ascension-day,* with its imagery of the New Jerusalem:

> I walk the fields of Bethani which shine
> All now as fresh as Eden, and as fine.
> Such was the bright world, on the first seventh day,
> Before man brought forth sin, and sin decay;
> When like a Virgin clad in flowers and green
> The pure earth sat, and the fair weeds had seen
> No frost, but flourish'd in that youthful vest,
> With which their great Creator had them drest;
> When Heav'n above them shin'd like molten glass,
> While all the Planets did unclouded pass;
> And Springs, like dissolv'd Pearls their streams did pour
> Ne'r marr'd with floods, nor anger'd with a showre.
>
> (ll. 37-48)

Even more clearly in the following *Ascension-Hymn,* Vaughan links the Old Eden and the New Paradise at the eschaton, brought to fulfillment through Christ, the Second Adam, "The Fuller whose pure blood did flow to make stain'd man more white than snow":

> Man of old
> Within the line
> Of Eden could
> Like the sun shine
> All naked, innocent and bright,
> And intimate with Heav'n, as light;
>
> But since he
> That brightness soil'd
> His garments be
> All dark and spoil'd
> And here are left as nothing worth,
> Till the Refiners fire breaks forth.

---

[33] *Discourses on Divers Texts of Scripture,* I, XXXV, cited in the Hughes edition of John Milton, 42.

Then comes he!
Whose mighty light
Made his cloathes be
Like Heav'n, all bright;
The Fuller, whose pure blood did flow
To make stain'd man more white than snow.

Hee alone
And none else can
Bring bone to bone
And rebuild man,
And by his all subduing might
Make clay ascend more quick than light.

(ll. 19-42)

The nostalgic yearning to return to the innocence of Paradise is a very common theme in seventeenth-century literature, with its longing for the New Age of Gold, when the sin and misery of the contemporary world will disappear in the perfection of the New Paradise.

Thomas Traherne equates the innocence of childhood with the innocence of the Garden, maintaining that childlike innocence is man's natural endowment just as it was in Paradise before the Fall. "Certainly Adam in Paradise", he says, "had not more sweet and curious apprehensions of the World, than I when I was a child."[34] As a child, he says:

I saw all in the Peace of Eden; Heaven and Earth did sing my Creators Praises and could not make more melody to Adam, than to me. All time was Eternity and a perpetual Sabbath ... The citie seemed to stand in Eden, or to be built in Heaven.[35]

The typological relationships of Childhood and Paradise recur throughout the poetry as well. In *Eden*, he says:

I knew not that there was a Serpents Sting,
Whose Poyson shed
On Men, did overspread
The World: Nor did I Dream of such a Thing
As Sin; in which Mankind lay Dead.

(ll. 8-12)

...

Only what Adam in his first Estate,
Did I behold ...

(ll. 29-30)

[34] *Century*, III, 1, *Centuries, Poems and Thanksgivings*, ed. H. M. Margoliouth (Oxford: At the Clarendon Press, 1958), II, 110.
[35] *Century*, III, 2, 3, pp. 110-111. All subsequent references to Traherne are from the two volume Margoliouth edition. The theme of regeneration is very rich in typological overtones, and there is considerable area for further investigation into this particular manifestation of seventeenth-century typology.

Those Things which first his Eden did adorn,
My Infancy
Did crown.
      (ll. 36-38)

Equating Paradise and Childhood, the poet is then a Second Adam:

That Prospect was the Gate of Heav'n that Day
The ancient light of Eden did convey
Into my Soul: I was an Adam there,
A little Adam in a Sphere
Of Joys ...
      (*Innocence*, ll. 49-53)

Or another Eve:

As Eve
I did believ
My self in Eden set ...
      (*Apostasy*, ll. 19-21)

In his *Meditations on the Six Days of the Creation*, in the poem on the
Sixth Day, Traherne pictures Paradise in terms of the Golden Age:

The earth was all throughout as Eden fair;
...
The harmless Lion with the Lamb did play,
And Leopards on the Sheep did never prey;
There nothing was that did destroy:
There nothing was that did annoy:
But all was love, and perfect Harmony;
All did the Maker's Goodness testify.
      (ll. 7, 19-24)

This is the Paradise of Childhood, the type of the innocence of the Garden
before the Fall, and an echo of Milton's "Paradise Within".

The Garden imagery in Marvell is a much more complicated thing.
The typological correspondences are not as clear cut, nor as carefully
worked out, and the border line between typological image and biblical
allusion is not easy to discern. Marvell does not give us any obvious
clues as to his use of type and figure, and as a result, no definitive con-
clusions can be reached. Empson, for example, has indicated the Paradise
imagery in Marvell's *The Garden*.[36] Marvell himself seems quite explicit
in Stanza VIII:

[36] "Marvell's Garden", in: William Empson, *Some Versions of Pastoral* (New York:
New Directions, 1960), 113-139. See also L. W. Hyman, "Marvell's Garden", *ELH*
XXV (1958), 13-22; Frank Kermode, "The Argument of Marvell's Garden", *Essays
in Criticism*, II, 1952.

> Such was the happy Garden-state,
> When Man there walk'd without a Mate:
> After a Place so pure, and sweet,
> What other Help could yet be meet:
> But 'twas beyond a Mortal's share
> To wander solitary there:
> Two Paradises 'twere in one
> To live in Paradise alone.
>
> (ll. 57-64)

But Empson himself succumbs to the danger of over-reading when he says that, "The bird (l. 53) is the dove of the Holy Spirit and carries a suggestion of the rainbow of the Covenant".[37] This is subjective typology at its worst.

One can make a case for typological references in *The Nymph Complaining for the Death of Her Faun*, with its background in the *Canticle of Canticles*, but there is little in the poem to support any explicit typological images.[38] There is a more explicit reference in *The Coronet*:

> Alas I find the Serpent old
> That twining in his speckled breast
> About the flow'rs disguised does fold,
> With wreathes of Fame and Interest,
> Ah, foolish Man, that wouldst debase with them,
> And mortal Glory, Heavens Diadem!
> But thou who only couldst the Serpent tame,
> Either his slippery knots at once untie,
> And disentangle all his winding snare ...
>
> (ll. 13-21)

In this passage there are echoes of Genesis 3:15 and Ambrose's comment about "the selfsame knots that were tied in condemnation are now undone".[39]

The Mower poems of Marvell may actually be structured on a typological theme, though it is difficult to point out anything more than hints of a typological structure. It seems quite possible that in *The Mower's Song* Juliana is an Eve type, bringing death and destruction, and the Meadows are a type of Paradise. But Marvell, in general, defies

---

[37] Empson, "Marvell's Garden", 121.

[38] See D. C. Allen, "Marvell's 'Nymph'", *ELH*, XXIII (1956), 93-111; Leo Spitzer, "Marvell's 'Nymph Complaining for the Death of Her Faun': Sources versus Meaning", *MLQ*, XIX (1958). There is much work still to be done on Marvell's use of the bible, and especially his use of implicit and explicit typological images. Marvell is a much more complicated poet than many other seventeenth-century authors, and his use of typology is correspondingly more difficult to unravel.

[39] Ambrose, *Expos. in Lucam*, IV, 7, *PL* 15:1614.

accurate categorization as a typological poet. There are enough indications to support the thesis that Marvell does make use of typological
themes in many of his poems, but if this is true, he certainly has taken
typology one step beyond its explicit use in poets like Milton and Herbert.

Donne's *Anniversary* poems sum up the three themes that have been
seen thus far — the typological references to Eve, Mary, and the Garden.[40]
For it would seem that Donne's two *Anniversary* Poems can be understood most simply as basically typological, and thus avoid the complica-
tions of many of the critics. The poems operate on many levels of typological correspondence, with complicating interrelationships between
the types. The poems are about Elizabeth Drury, but they are also about
the Blessed Mother and also about Queen Elizabeth.[41] At any given point
in the poems it is difficult to tell which of the three is the subject, for in a
sense, all three are. And all three are antitypes, in varying degrees of Eve,
the first Woman, for all three are *forma perfectior* of the pattern typified
by Eve.

There is an evident Christic correspondence in the typological relationships, too, for in Donne's praise of the three antitypes of Eve, they
themselves in their own turn are types of the Greater Christ. Donne
concludes the *Second Anniversary*:

> ... nor wouldst thou be content,
> To take this, for my second yeares true Rent,
> Did this Coine beare any other stampe, then his,
> That gave thee power to doe, me, to say this.
> Since his will is, that to posteritie,
> Thou shouldst for life, and death, a patterne bee,
> And that the world should notice have of this,
> The purpose, and th' authoritie is his;
> Thou art the Proclamation; and I am
> The Trumpet, at whose voyce the people came.
> (*SA*, ll. 519-528)

She is the Proclamation, the type of Christ. Coffin says that: "Though
Christ is not named in either of the *Anniversaries*, He is definitely figured
forth as Elizabeth Drury."[42] Further on he comments:

This is the heavy burden of religion and philosophy shouldered upon the
fragile story of the life and death of Elizabeth Drury. Unless we recognize in

---

[40] John Donne, *The Anniversaries*, ed. Frank Manley (Baltimore: John Hopkins
Press, 1963). See the discussion of the poems in Marjorie Hope Nicolson, *The Breaking
of the Circle*, revised edition (New York: Columbia University Press, 1960) and Louis I.
Martz, "John Donne in Meditation: *The Anniversaries*", *ELH*, XIV (1947), 247 ff.
[41] Marjorie Hope Nicolson, *The Breaking of the Circle*, 86.
[42] Charles Monroe Coffin, *John Donne and the New Philosophy* (New York, 1938), 258.

her brief encounter with human experience the lofty parallel to the Incarnation of Christ himself, Donne's attempt is hopeless ...[43]

Martz agrees with this analysis: "Donne here attempts to treat the girl in the convention of profane poetry of compliment, at the same time giving her the powers of a Christ."[44] Empson's conclusion is in the same vein:

Only Christ would be enough; only his removal from the world would explain the destruction foretold by astronomers. The only way to make the poem sensible is to accept Elizabeth Drury as the Logos.[45]

There is, indeed, another way to make the poem sensible, and that is to see *The Anniversaries* as basically typological. Thus Elizabeth Drury is not only a type of Christ, but also of Mary and of Elizabeth: Elizabeth herself is a type of Mary; and Eve, the First Woman, is a type of the Ideal Woman reflected in Elizabeth Drury, Elizabeth, and most perfectly in Mary, the Second Eve.

Jonson's remark that the *Anniversarie* poems "were prophane and full of blasphemies; that he told Mr. Donne if it had been written of the Virgin Marie it had been something; to which he answered that he described the Idea of Woman, and not as she was", indicates the basic intent and structure of the poems.[46] Donne is writing typologically, describing the Ideal Woman, as she appears in the three types of Mary, Elizabeth and Elizabeth Drury. Anthony Stafford has a similar remark, commenting that the Blessed Mother was "... not to be considered as a meere Woman, but as a Type, or an Idea, of an accomplished Piety".[47] Mary is the central antitype, then, and the others are all seen in the light of her perfection.

The First Woman, Eve, Mother of all the living, frustrates God's purpose and brings sickness into the world. "Woman, sent for man's reliefe" is made "cause of his languishment".

> For that first marriage was our funerall:
> One woman at one blow, then kill'd us all,
> And singly, one by one, they kill us now.
>
> (*FA*, ll. 101-107)

[43] Charles Monroe Coffin, 276.
[44] Louis I. Martz, "John Donne in Meditation: *The Anniversaries*", 247.
[45] William Empson, *English Pastoral Poetry* (New York: W. W. Norton, 1938), 84.
[46] Ben Jonson, "Conversation with Drummond", in: *Works* ed. C. H. Herford and P. Simpson (Oxford: Clarendon Press, 1947), I, 133.
[47] *The Femall Glory: or the Life and Death of Our Blessed Lady, the Holy Virgin Mary, God's Owne Immaculate Mother*, 1635, 177.

But the Fall of Eve is reversed in the antitype "Shee", who recapitulates and perfects the actions of the first Eve:

> She, of whom th'Ancients seem'd to prophesie,
> When they call'd vertues by the name of shee;
> Shee in whom vertue was so much refin'd,
> That for Allay unto so pure a minde
> Shee took the weaker Sex; shee that could drive
> The poysonous tincture, and the staine of Eve,
> Out of her thoughts and deeds; and purifie
> All, by a true religious Alchymie.
>
> (*FA*, ll. 174-182)

The two passages are related as type and antitype; the antitype is Mary, but it is also Elizabeth Drury and Elizabeth, the Queen.

The types are also linked by the fact that "shee" died, "cloathed in her virgin white integritie". Mary and Eve are Virgins in the patristic tradition. So are Elizabeth Drury and Queen Elizabeth.

Donne's linking of the reigning queen and the Blessed Mother was not unique in seventeenth-century poetry.[48] Jonson used the same typological reference of First and Second Mary in *An Epigram to the Queene, then Lying In* in 1630:

> Haile Mary, full of Grace, it once was said,
> And by an Angell, to the blessed'st Maid,
> The Mother of Our Lord: why may not I
> (Without prophaneness) yet, a Poet, cry
> Haile Mary, full of honours, to my Queene,
> The Mother of our Prince?[49]

Miss Nicolson has indicated another typological link between the three subjects of the *Anniversary* poems in Astraea, the mythical Virgin whose return will signal the Golden Age.

As Christians read Virgil's compliment to an unborn child into a prophecy of the coming of Christ, so they found in Astraea-Virgo, an anticipation of the Virgin Mary, as Donne suggests ...[50]

There is a final correspondence between the types in Church and Spouse imagery. Shee "... by a faithful confidence, was here / Bethroth'd to God, and now is married there".[51] She is also the Ark, in its own right a type of the Church:

[48] Elkin Wilson, *England's Eliza* (Cambridge: Harvard University Press, 1939), 215.
[49] Johnston edition, 206. See also Milton's *Sonnet* IX with its typological references to Mary, Ruth, and the Parable of the Virgins.
[50] *The Breaking of the Circle*, 96. For the discussion of the Astraea-Mary-Elizabeth-Drury linking, see pp. 91ff.
[51] *SA*, ll. 461-462. See also M. Bewley, "Religious Cynicism in Donne's Poetry", *KR*,

> Shee, who if those great Doctors truly said
> That the Ark to mans proportions was made,
> Had been a type for that, as that might be
> A type of her in this, that contrary
> Both Elements and Passions liv'd at peace
> In her, who caus'd all Civill war to cease.
>
> (*FA*, ll. 316-322)

Donne concludes in the final section of the *Second Anniversary*:

> Up, up, my drowsie Soule, where thy new care
> Shall in the Angells song no discord heare;
> Where thou shalt see the blessed Mother-Maid
> Joy in not being that, which men have said.
> Where she is exalted more for being good,
> Then for her interest of Mother-hood.
> Up to those Patriarchs, which did longer sit
> Expecting Christ, then they have enjoyed him yet.
> Up to those Prophets, which now gladly see
> Their Prophesies grown to be Historic.
> Up to the Apostles, who did bravely runne
> All the suns course, with more light then the Sonne.
> Up to those Martyrs, who did calmly bleed
> Oyle to th' Apostles Lamps, dew to their feed.
> Up to those Virgins, who thought, that almost
> They made joyntenants with the Holy Ghost,
> If they to any should his Temple give.
>
> (*SA*, ll. 339-355)

The passage summarises the typological fulfillment which is Donne's basic theme.

Donne writes 'strong lines' and he is not writing on a professedly biblical theme, as did Milton, Herbert, and others in the century. His typology is therefore much more involved and complicated, but the themes are all there in the *Anniversary* poems. The problem is to unravel the tangled strands of Donne's thought as it weaves its way through the overlapping images.

XIV (1952), 619-646 where he equates Elizabeth Drury and the Church in the Anniversary poems.

VIII

EXODUS TYPOLOGY

> Only to paraphrase the History of this Delivery, without
> amplifying, were furniture and food enough for a medita-
> tion ...
>
> John Donne, *Essays in Divinity*.

In the Twelfth Book of *Paradise Lost*, the Archangel Michael retells the
story of the Exodus of the Chosen People from Egypt, their wanderings
in the desert, and their final return "through the world's wilderness" to
the "eternal Paradise of Rest".[1] This story of the Exodus has always been
interpreted typologically in the history of Christian exegesis, and Milton
himself says that God on Sinai teaches the Chosen People by "types and
shadows" and disciplines them to a better Covenant, "from shadowy
Types to Truth, from Flesh to Spirit".[2] Isaiah used the Exodus events
typologically when he prophesied the New Exodus:

I am the Lord, your Holy One, the creator of Israel, your King. Thus saith the
Lord who made a way in the sea and a path in the mighty waters; Who brought
forth the chariot and the horse, the army and the strong. They lay down to
sleep together, and they shall not rise again: they are broken as flax and are
extinct. Remember not former things and look not on things of old. Behold
I do new things, and they shall spring forth. Verily, you shall know them. I
will make a way in the wilderness and rivers in the desert. The beast of the
field shall glorify me ... because I have given waters in the wilderness, rivers in
the desert, to give drink to my people, to my chosen.[3]

Paul uses the same typology in his exhortation to the Corinthians. After
recounting the events of the desert wanderings, Paul says that "these
things were done in a figure of us". They happened to our ancestors in a
figure and were "written for our correction", as a warning to us, "upon
whom the ends of the world are come".[4] This basic typological rela-

---

[1] Milton's account of the Exodus is in *P.L.*, XII, 155-314.
[2] *P.L.* XII, 302-303.
[3] Isaiah 43:16-20.
[4] I Cor. 10:1-12.

tionship became the basis for a whole set of varied and overlapping typological images in the early Church and in the interpretations of the Fathers. The Exodus of the Angel in passing over the first born of the Jews because they were marked with blood of the Lamb, and the Exodus of the Chosen People out of captivity in Egypt and through the Red Sea and the desert to the Promised Land under the leadership of Moses and Joshua, were just two of the themes that were used. The water from the rock, the brazen serpent, the manna, the cloud, the Covenant on Sinai, Moses himself, Joshua — all were typological figures of events to be fulfilled and perfected in the New Testament and for the people of the New Israel.[5]

The concept of the New Israel was a common image in the literature of the seventeenth century, with all of the accompanying overtones of the Exodus typology. The triple relationship of the Chosen People, Christ, our Passover, and the New People of God, was a fundamental relationship in the tradition of Exodus exegesis.

Universal Christian tradition has seen, in the people, events and institutions of the Exodus types of the New Testament and the Sacraments of the Church. There is a very evident continuity between the first-born of the Jews, saved by the avenging angel because they were marked with the blood of the lamb, Christ the firstborn of the new creation, conqueror of death through his blood, the blood of the true Lamb, and the Christian saved from the death due to sin because he was marked at Baptism with the blood of the Lamb. The continuity is emphasized by the coincidence of time between Christ's death and the anniversary of the Jewish Passover, and of Christian Baptism with the anniversary day of Christ's death.[6]

The seventeenth century made much of the relationship between the Chosen People and the Church of God, on both the theological and literary level. Davies remarks that Calvin "rediscovered the sense of the Church as the New Israel, the people of God",[7] and Donne uses the same typological relationship in his *Devotions*:

From that people to whom thou appearedst in signs and types, the Jews, thou art departed, because they trusted in them; but from thy Church, to whom thou hast appeared in thyself, in thy men, thou wilt never depart, because we cannot trust too much in him.[8]

---

[5] See for example, J. Guillet, "La Thème de la marche au désert dans l'Ancien et le Nouveau Testament", *Rech. Sc. Rel.* (1949), 164ff.

[6] Danielou, *From Shadows to Reality*, 153. See also Madsen, *From Shadowy Types to Truth*, 20-48.

[7] Horton Davies, *The Worship of the English Puritans* (London: Dacre Press, 1948), 20.

[8] *Devotions*, 130-131.

He repeats the same notion in his *Essays in Divinity*, as indicated by Simpson's lengthy note on the passage:

The flatness of the ending of the essays proper is redeemed by the four prayers which follow. The first of these gives us the key to the second part of the book. Donne's interest in the story of the Exodus is three-fold. First we have his prosaic and rather wearisome discussion of the details of the history. Secondly, as he has already indicated, there is the allegorical [typological] meaning, which had been fully worked out by the Fathers and the commentators from hints found in the New Testament. They saw the Exodus as a foreshadowing of the deliverance of the Church ("the Israel of God," as St. Paul calls it) from the slavery of the devil, through the Red Sea of Christ's blood, followed by the Wilderness of persecution, into the Promised Land. This interpretation has been constantly in Donne's mind throughout the book, as when he speaks of the devil as "That great Pharaoh, whose Egypt all the world is by usurpation," and continues "And then comest Thou, O Christ, thine own Moses, and deliveredst us; not by doing, but suffering; not by killing, but dying." The third interpretation arises out of the second, but it shifts the scene of the action from history to the individual soul. Here it is not the Church as a whole, but the soul of John Donne which has been in bondage to 'mine own corruption, mine own Pharaoh", and which is now in the wilderness of 'a more solitary and desert retiredness." Here at least we feel a link with the Holy Sonnets, where the spiritual conflict is described. In this first prayer, Donne finds in his own heart "Legions of spirits of Disobedience, and Incredulity and Murmuring," and implores God to overpower the wilfulness and stubborness which he himself is unable to remove. Compare this with Holy Sonnets II and XIV throughout.[9]

Milton also makes frequent use of the Exodus typology, identifying the Chosen people and the people of the Church. In the *Animadversions* he speaks of "... standing on the shore of that Red Sea into which our enemies had almost driven us", and many times in the pamphlets he uses the Exodus imagery to describe the rebellion against Charles, and expresses his hope that England will be a new Israel, a new Chosen People.[10]

The traditional interpretation of the Exodus types identified the Chosen People not only with the Church, but also with the individual soul, marked with blood of the Paschal Lamb at Baptism. Sandys uses this relationship in a Sermon Preached Before the Queen:

The Chiefest benefit which the Lord poured upon his people, and the first whereby he allured them to seek him was this: with an outstretched arm he brought them forth from the land of Egypt, the house of bondage, where their dwelling place was a prison, and a long life, long misery ... The like benefit

---

[9] *Essays in Divinity*, 96.
[10] Frye, "The Typology of Paradise Regained", 233.

in as great a measure of love, favour and power, we have received at the hands of our merciful God ... He hath delivered us from the tyranny and thralldom of that great Pharaoh, from Satan, our Moses, our great Captain, Jesus Christ, who on the cross got the victory, spoiled our enemy, cancelled the writing of our bondage and servitude, brought us through the Red Sea, and by his blood-shed wrought our perfect and full deliverance.[11]

The passage is rich in recapitulative and typological relationships, framed in the context of the Exodus and the New Israel, chosen and delivered by God from the slavery of the New Egypt.

At the very beginning of the seventeenth century Edward Stephens speaks of the Exodus as a "mystical institution of thy divine conduct of Souls through the Wilderness of this world to the Coelestial Regions of rest".[12] In a sermon delivered before the King at Whitehall in 1615, Lancelot Andrewes presents the Exodus typology in all its implications:

You may see all this represented in the shadows of the Old Testament. There is a book there called Exodus, of Israel's *egredietur* out of Egypt. Therein they had Moses for their guide; and he led them to the borders of the Holy Land, and there he left them; to show "the Law brought nothing to perfection." (Heb. 7:19). Then comes Joshua, whom the Epistle to the Hebrews calls Jesus, (Heb. 4:8), the figure of ours here, and by his conduct they were led and put in possession of the land of promise. All this but in type of another Testament "after to be made," saith Jeremy, (Jer. 31:31); and "upon better promises," saith the Apostle, (Heb. 8:6); namely, our spiritual leading through this vale of vanity to the true land of promise, "the heavenly Jerusalem that is from above," (Gal. 4:26); whither this our Jesus undertakes to bring all those that will be guided by Him. Observe but the correspondence between the type and the truth. Moses, when he came to lead the people, found them how? "scattered over all the land of Egypt, to seek stubble for brick," (Exod. 5:12), to build him a city that sought the ruin of them all. Our case right the very pattern of it; when our Guide finds us wandering in vanity, picking up straws, things that shall not profit us; "seeking death in the error of our life," (Wis. 1:12), till we be so happy as to light into His guiding. Secondly, Moses was to them not alone *dux viae*, 'a guide for the way;' but when enemies came forth against them, *dux militiae*, 'a captain for the way.' Christ was so too, and far beyond Moses. For He made us way with the laying down of His life. (Isaiah 53:12) So did neither Moses nor Joshua. Would die for it, but He would open us a passage to the place He undertook to bring us to. Was *Dux*, a Guide, in His life; *Dux*, a Captain, in His death. Thirdly, Moses when they fainted by the way obtained in their hunger manna "from Heaven," (John 6:32), and in their thirst "water out of the rock for them." Christ is Himself the "true Manna;" Christ, the spiritual Rock. (1 Cor. 10:4) Whom He leads He feeds; carries Bethlehem about Him.[13]

[11]   *The Sermons*, 145-146.
[12]   W. Jardine Grisbrooke, *Anglican Liturgies of the Seventeenth and Eighteenth Centuries* (London: SPCK, 1958), 238.
[13]   *Nativity Sermons*, 165-167.

It is logical to suppose that this Exodus typology would occur in the sermons of the century because of their foundation in the scriptural traditions of the Fathers, but the imagery is also used by the poets and literary men of the century. A large part of Marvell's *Upon Appleton House*, for example, is framed in an Exodus context. In the Meadows passage in the poem (stanzas XLVII-LX), Marvell is saying that Life is an Exodus, that the biblical images of the Exodus story are a type of all human life. He sets the Exodus scene in stanza XLVII:

> And now to the Abyss I pass
> Of that unfathomable Grass,
> Where Men like Grashoppers appear,
> But Grashoppers are Gyants there:
> They, in there squeking Laugh, contemn
> Us as we walk more low then them:
> And from the Precipices tall
> Of the green spir's, to us do call.

The image is from the Book of Numbers, Chapter 13, where at the end of the desert journey, Moses sends twelve spies from the desert of Pharan to view the land of Canaan. The spies return and report: "And there we saw the giants, the sons of Anak: and we were in our own sight as grasshoppers, and so we were in their sight" (13:33). In stanza XLIX, Marvell says that:

> The tawny Mowers enter next;
> Who seem like Israelites to be,
> Walking on foot through a green Sea.
> To them the Grassy Deeps divide,
> And crowd a lane to either side.

The image is clearly that of the passage through the Red Sea. Further on, in stanza LX, bloody Thestylis cries:

> ... he call'd us Israelites;
> But now, to make his saying true,
> Rails rain for Quails, for Manna Dew.

The haycocks in stanza LV remind the poet of the pyramids of Egypt. The mown meadows in stanza LVI are a new creation:

> The world when first created sure
> Was such a Table rase and pure.

They are like an empty canvas of Lilly, or like the bullring in Madrid before the entrance of the bulls. The cattle in stanza LVII are reminiscent of Davenant's Universal Herd in the account of Creation in Gondibert

II, VI. Finally, there is a Flood which destroys all in stanzas LIX-LXI.

This is very sophisticated use of typology, but Marvell seems to be saying that the Meadows of Appleton House, as also perhaps the whole poem, are an image of life. The Meadows passage recreates the glory of creation, from innocence to evil, from Creation to the Flood. It is also the story of an Exodus, a passage from death to salvation, in which mankind repeats the story of the Chosen People through their wanderings in the desert to the Promised Land.

The same typological relationship appears in Vaughan's *The Law, and the Gospel*, where the first two stanzas represent type and antitype, the Chosen People of the Old Testament and those of the New Testament, in a context of Exodus imagery — Paran, Sinai, a firie Law, thunder and threats.

> Lord, when thou didst on Sinai pitch
> And shine from Paran, when a firie Law
> Pronounc'd with thunder, and thy threats did thaw
> Thy Peoples hearts, when all thy weeds were rich
> And Inaccessible for light,
> Terrour, and might,
> Now did poor flesh (which after thou didst weare),
> Then faint, and fear!
> Thy Chosen flock, like leafs in a high wind,
> Whisper'd obedience, and their heads Inclin'd.
>
> But now since we to Sion come,
> And through thy bloud thy glory see,
> With filial Confidence we touch ev'n thee;
> And where the other mount all clad in flame,
> And threatning Clouds would not so much
> As 'bide the touch,
> We Climb up this, and have too all the way
> Thy hand our stay,
> Nay, thou tak'st ours, and (which ful comfort brings)
> Thy Dove too bears us on her sacred wings.

In the third stanza, Vaughan extends the correspondence to the Law and the Gospel:

> O plant in me thy Gospel, and thy Law,
> Both Faith and Awe;
> So twist them in my heart, that over there
> I may as wel as Love, find too thy fear!

The typological parallelism between Sinai and Sion, the Chosen Flock and Us, is the basic structure of the poem, and the correspondences between the Old Testament and the New Testament are carefully spelled out in the poem. Although Vaughan stresses the *forma perfectior* of the antitype Gospel, he indicates the genuine value of the type itself. It serves a purpose, for we need both Fear and Love. The relationship between type and antitype, Law and Gospel, is essentially Christic, for it is Christ who is foreshadowed in the reference to the incarnation in 1.7, and who perfects the Law in the fulfillment of the Gospel. Poor flesh which then fainted and feared, now approaches with filial confidence.

Herbert uses the same basic structure in his poem *Decay*. The poem contrasts the Old Law and the New, the Chosen People of the Exodus and the Chosen soul of the New Covenant. The shadow is perfected and fulfilled in the New Testament antitype, and the final stanza hints at the eschatological fulfillment of the type, when "thy great love" return, "And calling Justice, all things burn".

> Sweet were the dayes, when thou dist lodge with Lot,
> Struggle with Jacob, sit with Gideon,
> Advise with Abraham, when thy power could not
> Encounter Moses strong complaints and mone;
> Thy words were then, Let me alone.
>
> One might have sought and found thee presently
> At some fair oak, or bush, or cave, or well:
> Is my God this way? No, they would reply;
> He is to Sinai gone, as we heard tell:
> List, ye may heare great Aarons bell.
>
> But now thou dost thy self immure and close
> In some one corner of a feeble heart;
> Where yet both sinne and Satan, thy old foes,
> Do pinch and straiten thee, and use much art
> To gain thy thirds and little part.
>
> I see the world grows old, when as the heat
> Of thy great love, once spread, as in an urn
> Doth closet up it self, and still retreat,
> Cold sinne still forcing it, till it return,
> And calling Justice, all things burn.

Herbert has subtly fused the Old and New Testament correspondences, and although there are no explicit indications of the typological relationships, the whole poem is structured on a basically typological image: "Sweet were the dayes when ... But now ..." It is great Aaron, the priest type of the Exodus, who links the Old and the New Covenant.

The typology of the Exodus is essentially Christological as Paul pointed out in Corinthians, and Moses, the great figure of the Exodus, is clearly a Christ type. Sandys says our Exodus and deliverance from the great

Pharaoh, Satan, is accomplished at the hands "of *our* Moses, our great Captain, Jesus Christ".[14] Paul had made the same correlation in I Corinthians 10:1ff. and Stephen's words in Ch. 7 of Acts presuppose a Moses-Christ typology. Milton uses this relationship in *Paradise Lost* and in *Paradise Regained*, as has been seen above.

> ... whose high office now
> Moses in figure bears, to introduce
> One greater, of whose day he shall foretell,
> And all the Prophets, in thir Age the times
> Of great Messiah shall sing.[15]

Donne says:

That Moses and Elias talkt with Christ in the transfiguration, both Saint Matthew and Saint Marke tell us, but what they talkt of onely S. Luke, *Dicebant excessum ejus*, says he, they talkt of his decease, of his death which was to be accomplished at Jerusalem. The word is of his Exodus, the very word of our *exitus*, his issue by death. Moses who in his Exodus had prefigured this issue of Our Lord, and in passing Israel out of Egypt through the Red Sea, had foretold in that actual prophesie, Christ passing of mankind through the sea of his blood. And Elias, whose Exodus and issue out of this world was a figure of Christs Ascension had no doubt a great satisfaction in talking with Our Blessed Lord *de excessu ejus*, of the full consummation of all this in his death, which was to be accomplished at Jerusalem.[16]

Donne here weaves several typological strains together. Christ is the fulfillment of Moses and of Elias; Christ's death, his own Exodus, is the "full consummation" of the Exodus of the Jewish people and brings about the Exodus of the Church and of the individual soul, "Christ passing of mankind through the sea of his blood".

Christ is not only a Second Moses, but in the scriptural and patristic tradition, He is also the antitype of Joshua.[17]

Here the naming of Joshua — Jesus is treated as prophetic event foreshadowing things to come. Just as Joshua and not Moses led the people of Israel into the promised land of Palestine, so the grace of Jesus, and not the Jewish Law, leads the "second people" into the promised land of eternal beatitude. The man who appeared as the prophetic annunciation of the still hidden mystery, *qui in hujus*

---

[14] Sandys, *The Sermons*, 145-146. The emphasis is mine.
[15] *P.L.* XII, 240-245 and *P.R.* I, 349-355. See also *De Doctrina Christiana*, XIV, 93 and Augustine, *De Civ. Dei* 10, 8, and 18, 11.
[16] *Devotions Upon Emergent Occasions* together with *Deaths Duell*, 184-185. Michael Drayton uses the same typological relationships throughout his *Moses: His Birth and Miracles*, 1604, *Works*, ed. J. William Hebel (Oxford: Basil Blackwell, 1961), Vol. III.
[17] See for example, Hebrews 4:8, 14 and also Tertullian *Adv. Marc.*, III, 16, 18; IV, 7; *Adv. Jud.*, 9, 10. Danielou summarizes the scriptural and patristic background in *From Shadows to Reality*, 229ff.

sacramenti imaginis parabatur, was introduced under the *figura* of the divine name. Thus the naming of Joshua — Jesus is a phenomenal prophecy or pre-figuration of the future Saviour; *figura* is something real and historical which announces something else that is also real and historical. The relation between the two events is revealed by an accord or similarity. Thus, for example, Ter-tullian says in *Adversus Marcionem* (V, 7): *Quae Pascha Christi, si non Pascha figura Christi per similitudinem sanguinis et pecoris Christi*? (How is Christ the Passover, except inasmuch as the Passover is a figure of Christ through the likeness of the saving blood and of the flock of Christ?)[18]

Milton translates this tradition of Joshua-Jesus typology almost literally in *Paradise Lost*:

> But Joshua whom the Gentiles Jesus call,
> His name and Office bearing, who shall quell
> The adversary Serpent, and bring back
> Through the worlds wilderness long wander'd man
> Safe to eternal Paradise of rest.
> (*P.L.*, XII, 310-314)

This correspondence provides a hint of Christ's own triumph in the desert in *Paradise Regained*, which is rich in Exodus imagery and types. Christ is a second Moses, as well as a second Joshua; he spends forty days in the desert as the chosen people wandered forty years in the desert; His baptism at the beginning of *Paradise Regained* is a type of the Exodus, and also of the Exodus of the Christian's Baptism.[19]

Frye indicates the impact of the Christ figures in the Exodus and their relationship to Milton's *Paradise Regained*:

Inside the story of Adam is the story of Israel, who falls from the Promised Land into the bondage of Egypt and Babylon. Besides being a second Adam, Christ is also a second Israel, who wins back, in a spiritual form, the Promised Land and its capital city of Jerusalem. In this capacity the story of the Exodus, or deliverance of Israel from Egypt, prefigures his life in the Gospels. Israel is led to Egypt through a Joseph; Christ is taken to Egypt by a Joseph. Christ is saved from a wicked king who orders a massacre of infants; Israel is saved from the slaughter of Egyptian first-born. Moses organizes Israel into twelve tribes and separates it from Egypt at the crossing of the Red Sea; Christ gathers twelve followers and is marked out as the Redeemer at his baptism in the Jordan (which the Israelites also later cross.) Israel wanders forty years in the wilderness; Christ forty days. The Israelites receive the Law from Mt.

---

[18]   Auerbach, "Figura", 29.
[19]   See Danielou's comments on the Exodus imagery in Matthew's account of the desert temptation. "The narrative of the temptation presents it as a true Exodus, in which the true Israel, both in the desert and on the mountain top, offers the contrast of his own fidelity to the waywardness of the first Israel in the desert of Sinai." — *From Shadows to Reality*, 159, also 157 ff.

Sinai; the Gospel is preached in the Sermon on the Mount, which in its structure is largely a commentary on the Decalogue. The Israelites are plagued by serpents and redeemed by a brazen serpent on a pole, also accepted as a prototype of the Crucifixion by Christ. The Israelites conquer the promised Land under "Joshua whom the Gentiles Jesus call" (i.e. Joshua and Jesus are the same word), corresponding to Christ's victory over death and hell, as in the Church's calendar Easter immediately follows the commemorating of the temptations in Lent.[20]

Christ as the Lamb of God, the antitype of the Lamb directed by God to be sacrificed on the Day of Exodus, is such a frequent typological theme in seventeenth-century literature as to be almost a commonplace. The typology of the Lamb was established by Paul, and especially by John in his account of the Crucifixion, where he applies the ritual directive "Thou shalt not break a bone of it" directly to Christ, thus identifying the sacrificial Lamb of the Exodus and the Lamb of God who is sacrificed on the Cross.[21] The Christ-Lamb identification begins among the Fathers as early as Justin who says: "The mystery of the lamb which God ordered you to sacrifice as the Passover was truly a type of Christ ..."[22] and the references to the lamb in patristic literature are literally beyond counting. The figure was early taken up in the liturgy of the Church, and the prayers of the Missal and Breviary are rich in the use of the lamb of the Exodus as a figure of the sacrificed Christ, and Christ's Blood as the antitype of the blood of the lamb which was the mark of salvation for the first born among the Jews in Egypt.

The lamb typology also occurs with great frequency in the Liturgies of the seventeenth century. It would have been a reference that was frequently repeated and used in the church services of the period, and a familiar concept to the seventeenth-century reader.[23] It would be almost impossible to indicate all the references to the Christ-Lamb typology in the poetry of the period. The Lamb of God, with its mystical implications, is one of Crashaw's favorite symbols for Christ.[24] It is also a frequent image in Donne. In Holy Sonnets XII ("Father, part of this double interest") Donne speaks of:

> This Lambe, whose death, with life and world hath blest,
> Was from the Worlds beginning slain ...

[20] Frye, "The Typology of Paradise Regained", 228-229.
[21] John 19:36 and the references to Exodus 12:46 and Numbers 9:12. See also the Baptist's clear identification of Christ as the Lamb of God in John 1:29.
[22] *Dial. Trypho*, c. 12.
[23] See Grisbrooke, ed., *Anglican Liturgies of the Seventeenth and Eighteenth Centuries*, *passim*.
[24] See Austin Warren, *Richard Crashaw*, 183.

and in Sonnet II ("Oh my blacke Soule") Donne refers to the blood of Christ which washes souls clean. In *A Litanie* there is the echo of the invocation from the liturgical Litany of the Saints: "O Lambe of God, which took'st our sinne ..." (St. XXVIII). In *Ascention*, Donne skillfully opposes the images of the Strong Ramme and the Mild Lambe as types of Christ:

> O strong Ramme, which hast batter'd heaven for mee,
> Mild Lambe, which with thy blood, hast mark'd the Path.[25]

To quote just one further example of the many that are available in the literature of the seventeenth century, Vaughan writes of the shepherds at the birth of Christ:

> ... now they find him out, and taught before
> That Lamb of God adore,
> That Lamb whose daies great Kings and Prophets wish'd
> And long'd to see, but miss'd.

The context is clearly one of Old Testament prefiguration, and fulfillment in the antitype of the New Testament.[26]

The image of the Lamb and of the Blood of the Lamb is a liturgical type, as well as a direct foreshadowing of Christ's passion and death. In fact, the whole Exodus story was a prefiguration of the liturgical fulfillments, in the Old Law, first of all, in the partial fulfillment of the Jewish liturgical celebration of the Passover Feast, and then more fully and perfectly in the Christian Passover, and the Liturgies of the Eucharist. The Manna in the desert was a clear type of the Eucharist, and Christ himself establishes the basis of this typological correspondence in the sixth chapter of John. Vaughan uses this sacramental typology of the Lamb and the Manna of the Exodus as the framework of his "Admonitions, with Meditations and Prayers to be used before we come to the Lord's Supper" in *The Mount of Olives*.[27]

Danielou points out that the eating of the Manna, and the Paschal Lamb were types of the Eucharist, and that the Exodus itself, the crossing of the Red Sea and the Passage to the Promised Land, was a type of Baptism.[28] Cyril of Jerusalem summarizes the patristic tradition on the Exodus as a type of Christian Baptism:

---

[25] See the comment on this passage in Gardner, *Divine Poems*, 64. The Ramme type is from Micah 2:13.
[26] *The Shepheards*, ll. 46-50.
[27] *Works*, ed. L. C. Martin, 155-159. Similarly see Grisbrooke, *Anglican Liturgies*, 47-48.
[28] *From Shadows to Reality*, 175.

You must know that this type is found in ancient history. For when that cruel and ruthless tyrant Pharaoh oppressed the free and high-born people of the Hebrews, God sent Moses to bring them out of the evil thralldom of the Egyptians. The doorposts were anointed with the blood of the lamb, that the Destroyer might pass by those houses which had the sign of the blood. And so the Hebrew people were marvelously delivered. ... Now turn from the Ancient to the recent, from type to reality. There we have Moses sent from God to Egypt; here, Christ, sent by his Father into the world: There, Moses had to lead forth an oppressed people out of Egypt: Here, Christ rescues mankind when overwhelmed with sin; there, the blood of the lamb was the spell against the Destroyer: here the blood of the unblemished Lamb, Jesus Christ, puts the demons to flight: there, that tyrant pursued to the sea the people of God; and in like manner this brazen and shameless demon follows the people of God to the very water of salvation. The tyrant of Old was drowned in the sea, and the present tyrant is destroyed in the saving water.[29]

The Baptismal typology is continued in the crossing of the Jordan into the Promised land by the Jewish people.[30] But the Jordan typology was a very rich one, and was not limited to the actual Baptismal correspondence. As Tuve points out:

The Jordan whose crossing was already a symbol of redemption in the Old Testament became a yet more powerful one in the New, and the medieval Church widened and deepened its significances. As with many water symbols, its basic element is purification from sin, but its range of meanings becomes very great. The Chosen People, the Church of God, enter heaven and eternal life through the waters of Jordan; the single soul which in wedding Christ becomes his temple enters through its waters the joy of his eternal presence; its waters are the waters of Baptism and this is the water that flowed from Christ's side, the regenerating and fructifying water; Christ's Baptism and Epiphany are paralleled and these are one with the wedding of Christ with his Church or with the soul ... As Naaman was cleansed of his leprosy in the waters of Jordan, so Christ came to cleanse men from the leprosy of sin ... Jordan 'signifies Baptism.' This last is a commonplace occuring uncountable times in gloss and commentary.[31]

This typological image, as Miss Tuve has pointed out so well, is the basis

---

[29]   *Tractatus Mysteriorum, PG* 33:1068a. This Baptismal typology first appears in Paul, I Corinthians 10:1-11, but is frequently used in the Fathers. See, for example, Tertullian, *De Baptismo,* cc. 8-9, Ambrose, *De Mysteriis* and *De Sacramentis,* and Gregory of Nyssa, *The Life of Moses,* the *Commentary on the Song of Songs* and the *Catechetica Magna.* For further patristic references, cf. Jean Danielou, "Traversée de la Mer Rouge et Baptême aux premiers siècles", *Rech. Sc. Rel.* XXXIII (1946), 402-430.
[30]   See "The Crossing of the Jordan as a Type of Baptism", Danielou, *From Shadows to Reality,* 261-275.
[31]   Rosemond Tuve, *A Reading of George Herbert* (Chicago: University of Chicago Press, 1952), 184.

of Herbert's Jordan poems.[32] Although there is no direct reference in either of the poems to any of the biblical events of the Exodus, the whole structure of the two poems, and Herbert's use of the Jordan title, make it clear that they are poems of *regeneration*, of purification. They represent a New Baptism, the beginning of a New Life for the poet. He has crossed his own poetic Jordan, and has been purified in the saving waters of the Jordan. He has left the desert of the wandering, has turned his back on the fictions, the enchanted groves and the purling streams of the love poetry of the age. On another level, Herbert seems to be saying that his love has been purified by the passage of the Jordan. The unworthy or less worthy love of the poets who sing of 'lovers loves' and shepherds, has given way to the one true love, the love of God. Secular poetry has yielded to the divine. The desert journey is over and the Promised Land has been reached.[33] As Miss Tuve points out, in each of the Jordan poems, Herbert "makes a personal dedication of his imagination to Heavenly Love".[34]

It is quite clear that Jordan, Christian symbol of redemptive purification and of entrance into union with Christ as Heavenly Love incarnate, was Herbert's own symbol for this complex of ideas, and that he thought of poetry as both the means and the fruit of such a union. The symbol was a 'public' one. We have observed in Herbert's own poems its manifold and deep implications; it should be made clear that such a complex of metaphorical meanings was also 'public,' and no mere idiosyncracy, born of chance tie-ups between a number of Bible verses. Because it was public it was understood, and not only subtle but moving.[35]

Basically, the symbol is typological, and as such, carries the full weight of the event in the story of the Exodus and all the overtones of the fulfillment of the type in the perfected New Testament antitype. Miss Tuve then continues:

I have remarked upon the fundamental symbolic weight of 'Jordan', in the Old Testament and in the New, in connection with the sacrament of Baptism and with the promise of and the entrance into eternal life, in connection with Christ's Baptism and the soul or the Church as the Bride, especially when Baptism and Epiphany are paralleled. All of these are connexions implying regeneration, cleansing, dedication redemptive salvation; they are too commonplace to need illustration.[36]

---

[32]   Tuve, 182-203. Once again, in the *Jordan* poems of Herbert, we are presented with a typological theme that offers many possibilities for further investigation.
[33]   The commentary in the Hutchinson edition makes reference to all these typological references. See pp. 495, 513.
[34]   Tuve, *Reading of George Herbert*, 188.
[35]   Tuve, 197.
[36]   Tuve, 197.

It should be apparent that this "symbolic weight" in the Jordan poems is actually typological, and that the full force and meaning of the poems derives from the context of type — antitype relationships implied in the Exodus account of the crossing of the Jordan. The context is so obvious, that Herbert need refer to it only in the use of the *Jordan* title for the two poems. It was, indeed, a 'public' image, a typological correspondence that would have been immediately clear to the seventeenth-century reader.

Of all the seventeenth-century poets, George Herbert perhaps makes the greatest use of the Exodus typological themes. The images are constantly recurring throughout his poems, but in two of them especially, *The Bunch of Grapes* and *The Sacrifice*, he uses the themes of the Exodus to great effect. Summers says that:

... every event during the wandering of the children of Israel from Egypt to the Promised Land was a type of the Christian's experience in his journey between the world of sin and heaven ...[37]

Herbert has taken one small incident from the story of the Exodus, the cluster of grapes which the messengers brought back from the Promised Land in Numbers 13:23, and used it as a type of the Christian experience. Tuve has illustrated the tradition which saw in the Cluster of Grapes a figure of the inheritance of the Chosen People, crossing over Jordan into the Promised Land.[38] The commentary on the poem in the Hutchinson edition states the typological basis of the poem:

The story of the Israelites journeying from the Red Sea through the Wilderness to the Promised Land is also our story, because God's righteous acts are prophetic and foreshadow our case too. And if we do not meet with their "cluster of grapes" (Num. 13:23) we have Christ the "true vine" (John 15:1).[39]

The Exodus is the type of the poet's own wanderings in the desert. "I am where I began / Sev'n years ago ... I did towards Canaan draw; but now I am / Brought back to the Red Sea, the sea of shame." The journey of the Jews of old in the desert is the type of the Christian's journey, too: "Their storie pennes and sets us down." The Christians have their guardian fires and clouds, and their own Manna, sands and serpents, just as did the wandering Jews. But where, the poet asks, is the cluster of grapes? Where is the joy of deliverance? Where is the Promised

---

[37]   Joseph Summers, *George Herbert: His Religion and Art* (Cambridge: Harvard University Press, 1954), 127.
[38]   Tuve, *A Reading of George Herbert*, 112 ff. See also the Illustrations for the iconographical use of the same typological theme.
[39]   See p. 552.

Land? The fulfillment, he says, is far better than the type; the truth far outshines the image. "Can he want the grape, who hath the wine? / I have their fruit and more." The poem, brief and simple as it is, is a good example of Herbert's skill with typological images. If the typological correspondences are ignored, the poem loses almost all its meaning and power.

The image of the bunch of grapes suggests, then not only the foretastes of Canaan and heaven, but also the immeasureable distances between the foretastes under the Covenant of Works and the Covenant of Grace.[40]

A much more ambitious poem based on the Exodus typology is Herbert's *The Sacrifice*. Miss Tuve has analyzed the poem in some detail and there is little to add to her remarks concerning the typological symbolism.[41] The imagery of the poem is taken from the Breviary and the Liturgical services for Holy Week, particularly from the *Lamentations* of Jeremiah and the *Improperia* or Reproaches of the Good Friday Service. The Holy Week services themselves are full of Exodus typology, and Herbert has transferred almost all these types to his poem. Holy Week itself is the liturgical antitype of the historical Exodus, and both the liturgical type and the historical type in the Old Testament prefigure the Exodus of the Church and of the individual soul, while commemorating the Exodus of Christ in his Passion, death and resurrection.[42]

Herbert indicates his use of the *Lamentations* in the very first line of the poem: "O all ye, who pass by ..." and in his use of the recurring refrain: "Was ever grief like mine?" Donne has translated the familiar refrains from the Holy Week services in *The Lamentations of Jeremy, for the most part according to Tremelius*.[43] As Tuve has pointed out, the *Lamentations* were very familiar to the seventeenth century from the Matins of the last three days of Holy Week, and some of the best polyphonic music of the late sixteenth and seventeenth centuries was written for these liturgical uses.[44]

Herbert's second major source of imagery in the poem is the *Improperia* from the Adoration of the Cross in the Good Friday liturgical service. There are so many echoes of these *Improperia* in *The Sacrifice*, in both explicit and implicit references, that it would be a monumental

---

[40] Summers, *George Herbert*, 127.
[41] Tuve, *A Reading of George Herbert*, 19 ff. See also the discussion of the Sacrifice in William Empson, *Seven Types of Ambiguity* (New York: Meridian Books, 1963), 256 ff.
[42] Cf. the last nine poems of Herrick's *Noble Numbers* which form a Holy Week sequence. *The Poetical Works of Robert Herrick*, ed. L. C. Martin (Oxford: At the Clarendon Press, 1956), 398-403.
[43] Gardner, *Divine Poems*, 35 ff.
[44] Tuve, *A Reading of George Herbert*, 24-25.

task to list them all. The basic structure of the *Improperia* is typological, and the correspondence is between the historical Exodus of the Chosen People and the Exodus of Christ during his passion. The third source of imagery in the poem is obviously the Gospel account of the Passion and Death. Herbert actually follows the chronology of the Passion accounts, and uses the *Lamentations* as a constant refrain, and the *Improperia* exodus typology as his basic structural references. A comparison of the full text of the *Improperia* which follows, with *The Sacrifice* will indicate how deeply indebted Herbert is to the Liturgical prayer for his imagery.

Songs of Reproach

Antiphon I: My people, what have I done to you? or in what have I grieved you? Answer me. Because I brought you out of the land of Egypt, you have prepared a Cross for your Saviour.

Antiphon II: O Holy God. O holy mighty One. O holy immortal One, have mercy upon us.

Because I led you through the desert for forty years, and fed you with manna, and brought you into a land exceedingly good, you have prepared a cross for your Saviour.

Antiphon II. O Holy God ...

What more must I do for you, that I have not done? I planted you, indeed, my most beautiful vineyard, and you have become exceedingly bitter to me for in my thirst you gave me vinegar to drink, and with a spear you have pierced the side of your Savior.

Antiphon II: O Holy God ...

For your sake I scourged Egypt with its firstborn: and you have scourged me and delivered me up.

Antiphon I: My people ...

I brought you out of Egypt having drowned Pharaoh in the Red Sea: and you have delivered me to the Chief Priests.

Antiphon I: My people ...

I opened the sea before you: and you with a spear have opened my side.

Antiphon I: My people ...

I went before you in a pillar of cloud: and you have brought me to the Judgment hall of Pilate.

Antiphon I: My people ...

I fed you with Manna in the desert: and you have beaten me with blows and scourges.

Antiphon I: My people ...

I gave you the water of salvation from the rock to drink: and you have given me gall and vinegar.

Antiphon I: My people ...

For you I struck the kings of the Canaanites: and you have struck my head with a reed.

Antiphon I: My people ...

I gave you a royal scepter: and you have given to my head a crown of thorns.

Antiphon I: My people ...

I have exalted you with great power: and you have hanged me on the gibbet of the cross.

Antiphon I: My people ...

Antiphon III: We adore your Cross, O Lord, and we praise and glorify your holy resurrection: for behold, by the wood of the cross joy came into the whole world.

Psalm 66: O God, be gracious, and bless us; and let your face shed its light upon us, and have mercy on us.

Antiphon III: We adore your cross ...[45]

In *The Sacrifice*, Herbert is clearly using Moses as a type of Christ. Christ's face is veiled as was Moses': "As Moses face was vailed, so is mine" (l. 137). Moses struck the rock in the desert to bring forth water; Christ's head is struck with the reed:

> They strike my head, the rock from whence all store
> Of heav'nly blessings issue evermore.
>   (ll. 169-170)

The same image is complicated in Herbert's Moses-Caesar-Christ equation:

> Why, Caesar is their onely king, not I:
> He clave the stonie rock, when they were drie;
> But surely not their hearts, as I well trie;
> Was ever grief like mine?
>   (ll. 121-124)

Christ is the *forma perfectior*, relating to Moses *per idem*, but in more perfect fulfillment, and to Caesar *per contrarium*. The imagery is complicated, but clearly typological. Herbert is identifying Christ, our great Captain, with Moses and the Exodus.

[45] *Saint Andrew Bible Missal* (Bruges, Belgium: Biblica, 1960), 463-465.

No cleric of the seventeenth century as liturgically literate as George Herbert, and brought up on typology, could mention this act of Moses without thinking both of the water from the side of Christ, the living rock (l. 170) and the mystical regenerative power of water, so stressed for example in the service for Easter Even. ... Whole stanzas of Herbert's poem gain their compressed force from that acceptance of Moses as a type of Christ ... This typological parallel, especially the specific element in it used in the stanza quoted, was *within not outside* the poem to Herbert and his generation. This is not only because it had been a commonplace of biblical commentary for centuries, but because the rock struck by Moses is allegorized as referring to Christ in I Cor. 10:4, and because it is one of the commonest of all iconographical symbols of the sacraments issuing from the side of Christ the living rock ... And the typological identification of Christ with Moses — common to all the materials Herbert echoes — was assuredly in the author's mind, if that makes any odds to our reading. And if it does not make any odds, I submit that we are stubborn readers.[46]

There are further references to Exodus typology throughout the poem· Christ's words: "I give them bread" in line 7, echoes the Manna of the Desert and his own prediction of Living Bread in John 6. Christ is the "meak and readie Paschal Lamb of this great week" (ll. 58-59), who rescues the Chosen people from slavery in Egypt (l. 10). Isaiah's Parable of the Vineyard, with its typological implications as it occurs in the *Improperia*, underlines the paradox of the Exodus story:

> Then on my head a crown of thorns I wear:
> For these are all the grapes Sion doth bear,
> Though I my vine planted and watered there.
>
> (ll. 161-163)

There are other typological themes in the poem in addition to the Exodus figures. Christ is a second Adam (l. 70) and there is an implied reference to the Second Eve in:

> For they will pierce my side, I full well know:
> That as sinne came, so Sacraments might flow.
>
> (ll. 246-247)

Christ is a second Noah:

> My dove doth back into my bosom flie,
> Because the raging waters still are high.
>
> (ll. 94-95)

And by his Exodus Christ inaugurates a Second Creation:

> Lo, here I hang, charg'd with a world of sinne,
> The greater world 'o the two; for that came in
> By words, but this by sorrow I must win.
>
> (ll. 205-207)

---

[46]　Tuve, *A Reading of George Herbert*, 28-30.

The New Creation is accomplished by Christ's recapitulative action as the
Second Adam reversing the Fall of our First Parents:

> So sits the earths great curse in Adams fall
> Upon my head: so I remove it all
> From th'earth unto my brows, and bear the thrall:
> Was ever grief like mine?
>   (ll. 165-168)
>
> ...
>
> O all ye who passe by, behold and see;
> Man stole the fruit, but I must climbe the tree;
> The tree of life to all but me;
> Was ever grief like mine?
>   (ll. 201-204)

Christ is the Antitype of all these Old Testament figures — Adam, Noah,
Moses — and his Exodus is at once the fulfillment of the historical Exodus, and at the same time the pledge of the Exodus of the individual
Christian from death to life. Christ is the *forma perfectior*, in his own
words which echo the patristic imagery:

> How with their lanterns do they seek the sunne!
>   (l. 35)

IX

"JACOB'S PILLOW AND PILLAR": NOAH AND TEMPLE TYPOLOGY

> As his manner is, the Psalmist ... under one compriseth the type and the truth both; by these things which befell the people of the Jews, the Church typical, shadowing out those things which were to befall the Antitype of it, Christ and his Church.
>
> Lancelot Andrewes, *Nativity Sermons.*

Henry Vaughan has fused several typological themes in his poem *Jacob's Pillow and Pillar,* using all the elements of type and antitype in his retelling of the story of Jacob's sleep and vision in Genesis 28:10-22.[1] Jacob himself states the basic typological theme when he says:

Indeed, the Lord is in this place, and I knew it not ... How terrible is this place: This is no other but the house of God, and the gate of heaven ... And this stone which I have set up for a title shall be called the House of God ...[2]

Jacob's pillar is a type of the Temple, and just as God dwells in this "terrible" place, so He will dwell in the temple — the actual historical temple of Solomon, and the temple of the individual soul. Vaughan says: "I see the Temple in the Pillar rear'd ..." (l.1), and: "Thus is the solemn temple sunk agen / Into a Pillar ..." (ll. 35-36). The Pillar is but a type, a shadowy prefiguration of the greater antitype which is to come:

> And that dread glory, which thy children fear'd,
> In milde, clear vision, without a frown,
> Unto thy solitary self is shown.
> (ll. 2-4)
>
> ...
>
> The first true worship of the worlds great King
> From private and selected hearts did spring,
> But he most willing to save all mankinde,
> Inlarged that light, and to the bad was kinde.
> (ll. 11-14)

---

[1] *The Works of Henry Vaughan,* ed. L. C. Martin (Oxford: At the Clarendon Press, 1957), pp. 527-528.
[2] Genesis 28:16-17, 22.

Jacob's pillow was "like some common stone", but it becomes a Pearl "when once made publique" (ll. 17-18).

> This little Goshen, in the midst of night,
> And Satans seat, in all her Coasts hath light,
> Yea Bethel shall have Tithes (saith Israels stone)
> And vows and Visions, though her foes crye, None.
> Thus is the solemn temple sunk agen
> Into a Pillar, and concealed from men.
> And glory be to his eternal Name!
> Who is contented, that this holy flame
> Shall lodge in such a narrow pit, till he
> With his strong arm turns our captivity.
>   (ll. 31-40)

The Pillar is but a tiny reflection of the Temple to come, for Jacob stands a long way from the Day-star:

> And all that distance was Law and command.
> But we a healing Sun by day and night,
> Have our sure Guardian, and our leading light;
> What thou didst hope for and believe, we finde
> And feel a friend most ready, sure and kinde.
> Thy pillow was but type and shade at best,
> But we the substance have, and on him rest.
>   (ll. 48-54)

In these lines, there is also an implied typological link between Jacob himself and Christ. Jacob is also a shade and type, but we have the substance, "and on him rest". The same typological correspondence is implied in the earlier lines:

> But blessed Jacob, though thy sad distress
> Was just the same with ours, and nothing less;
> For thou a brother and blood-thirsty too
> Didst flye, whose children wrought thy children wo ...
>   (ll. 40-44)

The Jacob-Christ typology is not particularly common, but there are references to it in the Fathers, and Donne makes use of it in one of his sermons.[3]

Vaughan makes use of a second typological theme in *Jacob's Pillow and Pillar*, equating Noah's ark with the pillar of Jacob's vision, with the Temple, and the individual soul. He says that God foresaw that Man would slight his Maker, and He "foretold the place, and form to serve him in" (ll. 23-24). That place;

[3] See Justin, *Dial* 140:1, also Donne, *Sermons*, ed. Potter and Simpson, I, 278.

> ... should be true grace
> And the meek heart, not in a Mount, nor at
> Jerusalem, with blood of beasts and fat.
> A heart is that dread place, that awful Cell,
> That secret Ark, where the milde Dove doth dwell
> When the proud waters rage ...
>   (ll. 24-28)

Jacob's pillow and pillar is a type of the temple, the House of God and the Gate of Heaven, but it is also a type of the Ark of the heart, the Temple of the individual soul, where God is worshipped even after the historical temple is destroyed.

The Flood has always been one of the fundamental figures of biblical typology. The Ark was a type of the Christian's salvation, Noah a Christ figure, the rainbow a sign of the Covenant, the Flood itself a type of Christian Baptism. In the first Epistle of Peter, the Flood was treated as the type of Baptism,[4] and the Baptismal Rite in the Book of Common prayer, uses the Noah typology.

In the allegorical accounts of the Middle Ages Noah was always treated as one of the great precursors of the Saviour. Endless comparisons were made between the waters of the Flood and these of Baptism, between the wood of the Ark and the wood of the Cross, and between the door in the Ark and the wound in Christ's side. So the story of Noah had as definite a sanctity as the story of Adam, Samson, David, and any other of the great adumbrations of the doctrine of grace ...[5]

In Milton's account of the History of Salvation in the last two books of *Paradise Lost*, Abraham occupies just thirty-five lines, David thirty lines, and Moses less than a hundred lines, but the story of Noah and the Flood takes up some two hundred lines. As Allen comments:

It may be that Milton found the story of Noah more artistically attractive; and moreover it was always considered one of the best allegorical [typological?] adumbrations of the life and ministry of Christ.[6]

Donne uses this Baptismal-Salvation typology in the opening lines of *A Hymne to Christ, at the Authors last Going into Germany*:

> In what torne ship soever I embarke,
> That ship shall be my embleme of thy Arke;

---

[4] I Peter 3:20-21.

[5] Don Cameron Allen, *The Legend of Noah: Rennaissance Rationalism in Art, Science and Letters* (Urbana: University of Illinois Press, 1949), 138-139. In the patristic tradition, see Tertullian, *De Baptismo* 8, *PL* 1:1209; Cyprian, *PG* 23:85; Chrysostom, *PG* 48:1037. Also J. Danielou, "Déluge, baptême, jugement", *Dieu Vivant*, VIII (1947), 97-112, and *From Shadows to Reality*, 69-115.

[6] Allen, *The Legend of Noah*, 154.

> What sea soever swallow mee, that flood
> Shall be to mee an embleme of thy blood ...[7]

The word "embleme" is often used synonymously with type, and Donne is correlating the Ark and his own ship, the Flood and the Blood of Christ, the instrument of salvation. In the *First Anniversary*, Donne uses the tradition of the Ark as a type of the individual Christian:

> That the Arke to mans proportions was made ...
> (l. 318)

And in a sermon on Marriage, he says the Ark was "a type of our best condition in this life".[8]

The Flood was also considered a Second Creation, the antitype of the First Creation, and a further type of the final Creation to come with Baptism. Paul calls Baptism a παλιγγενεσία, a new Genesis, a regeneration, a new creation,[9] and Donne says: "In this first creation thus presented, there is a shadow, a representation of our second creation, or Regeneration in Christ."[10] In the *Second Anniversary*, he talks of the three births of the soul — at creation, the rebirth of Grace in Baptism, and the final birth in Heaven at the Resurrection.[11]

The Rainbow and the Covenant types of the Flood are also frequent themes in the literature of the period. Although there are no explicit typological links expressed in Vaughan's *The Rain-bow*, the typological correspondence is implied throughout the poem, with its emphasis upon the fulfillment and the perfection of the antitype in the New Testament:

> Still yong and fine! but what is still in view
> We slight as old and soil'd, though fresh and new.
> How bright were thou, when Shem's admiring eye
> Thy burnisht, flaming Arch did first descry!
> (ll. 1-4)

> When I behold thee, though my light be dim,
> Distant and low, I can in thine see him,
> Who looks upon thee from his glorious throne
> And mindes the Covenant 'twixt All and One.
> (ll. 15-18)

A final type in the Flood imagery is the relationship between the Ark

---

[7] Gardner, *Divine Poems*, 48.
[8] Gill, *Sacred Philosophy of Holy Scripture*, 74.
[9] Titus 3:5. See the Flood-Creation Correspondence in Marvell's *Upon Appleton House* discussed above in Chapter VIII.
[10] *Sermons*, ed. Potter and Simpson, I, 289.
[11] Line 215. The typological themes of creation and regeneration in seventeenth-century literature are very rich, and deserving of much fuller treatment than is possible within the confines of the present study.

and the Resurrection of Christ. Renaissance iconography made much of this relationship, picturing the Ark as a box, a sepulchre, from which Christ rises, as does the individual soul at the final moment of Judgment.

Noah is the premonstration of the Second Adam's victory and so the ark must look like a grave chest, like a sarcophagus, the funeral box in which the body of Christ was laid.[12]

Similar to this Christ-Noah typology in the resurrection, is the traditional interpretation of Jonah as a figure of Christ. Christ uses this 'Sign of Jonah' in reference to himself: "For as Jonah was in the belly of the whale for three days and three nights, so shall the Son of man be in the heart of the earth three days and three nights."[13] Bainton quotes this use of Christic typology and then concludes:

According to this mode of exegesis, the history of the Old Testament becomes as it were a symphony in which a theme is developed with variations, never with exact repetition, but with recognizable adaptations and perchance antitheses leading up to an ultimate resolution.[14]

A second theme in Vaughan's *Jacobs Pillow and Pillar* is the typology of the Temple. There is the historical temple of the Old Testament, but there is also the temple of the New Testament, the Church of God, and finally there is the temple of the individual soul. This temple typology is a very frequent theme in Paul. In Ephesians, he writes:

Now therefore you are no more strangers and foreigners: but you are fellow citizens with the saints and domestics of God; Built upon the foundation of the Apostles and prophets, Jesus Christ himself being the chief cornerstone: in whom all the building being framed together into a habitation of God in the Spirit.[15]

The relationship between the Temple and the individual soul is very clearly established in Corinthians:

Know you not that you are the Temple of God and that the Spirit of God dwelleth in you? But if any men violate the temple of God, him shall God destroy. For the Temple of God is holy, which you are ... For you are the Temple of the living God; as God saith: I will dwell in them and will walk among them, And I will be their God and they shall be my people.[16]

---

[12]   Allen, *Legend of Noah*, 156 and *passim*.
[13]   Matthew 12:40.
[14]   Roland H. Bainton, "The Bible in the Reformation", *The Cambridge History of the Bible: The West from the Reformation to the Present Day*, ed. S. L. Greenslade (Cambridge: Cambridge University Press, 1963), 25-26. For the patristic tradition of Jonah as a type of Christ, see Cyril of Jerusalem, *Cat.*, 14:20 and Theodore of Mopsuestia, *Comm. in Jonam, PG* 66:320-327.
[15]   *Ephesians* 2:19-22. See also 2:11 to 3:6.
[16]   I Corinthians 3:16-18; II Corinthians 6:16.

God is present in the individual soul, just as He was present in the temple of old, and it is this divine presence which provides the correspondence of similitude between the historical temple of the Old Testament as type, and the temple of the New Testament in the individual Christian as antitype. Christ is the cornerstone of both temples, as Paul indicates in I Corinthians 3; the typological link is essentially Christic. The temple is also a figure of the Church, of the Chosen People of the New Testament, the New Jerusalem. This relationship of temple and Church was implicit in the Eve-Mary-Church typology discussed above. After discussing the Church as the mystic Eve, Ambrose continues:

For the building of this city how many are sent by God: The patriarchs and the prophets, the Archangel Gabriel and countless angels — and the whole heavenly host gives praise to God because the perfection of the city draws nigh. Many are sent, it is true, but it is Christ alone who is the builder, though indeed he is not alone, for the Father is with Him. And if he is the only builder, yet he does not usurp to himself the glory of so great a labor. It is written of Solomon's Temple, which is a type of the Church, that when it was building there were seventy thousand men to carry the materials on their shoulders, eighty thousand stone cutters and three thousand six hundred overseers (II Par. 2:2). Let his angels come, then, heavenly stone cutters; let them cut off all that is superfluous in us and remove all roughness. Let them come and lift us on their shoulders, for it is written: "On their shoulders shall they be carried" (Isaiah 49:22).[17]

Ambrose here links the three elements of temple typology — the historical Temple of Solomon, the Church, and the individual soul. Origin summarizes the patristic tradition of temple typology as follows:

Those who observed the Law which foreshadowed the true Law, possessed a shadow of diverse things, a likeness of the things of God. In the same way, those who shared out the land that Juda inherited, were imitating and foreshadowing the distribution that will ultimately be made in heaven. Then the reality was in heaven, the shadow and the image of reality was on earth; there was an earthly Jerusalem, a temple, an altar, a visible liturgy, priests and high priests, towns and villages, too, in Juda and everything also that you find described in the book. But at the coming of the Lord Jesus Christ, when truth descended from heaven and was born on earth, and justice looked down from heaven (Ps. 84:12), shadows and images saw their last. Jerusalem was destroyed and so was the temple; the altar disappeared. Henceforth neither Mount Garizim nor Jerusalem was the place where God was to be worshipped; his true worshippers were to worship him in spirit and truth (Jn. 4:23). Thus, in the presence of the truth, the type and shadows came to an end, and when a temple was built in the Virgin's womb by the Holy Spirit and the power of the Most High (Luke 1:33), the stone temple was destroyed.[18]

[17]   *Expos. in Lucam*, 2, 89, *PL* 15:1668.
[18]   *Hom. Jos.*, 17:1.

Andrewes uses the basic temple typology in a sermon preached in 1615:

So we come to have two sorts of Temples. Temples of flesh and bone, as well as Temples of lime and stone. For if our bodies be termed houses, because our souls, tenantwise, abide and dwell in them; if because our souls dwell they be houses, if God do so they be temples: why not? ... But then they be so specially when actually we employ them in the service of God. For being in his temple, and there serving Him then if ever they be *Temple in Temple*, "living Temples in a Temple without life." A body then may be a Temple, even this of ours.[19]

Herbert's *The Temple* is certainly the best expression of this temple typology in the literature of the seventeenth century, and the themes were echoed in the poems which draw their inspiration from Herbert's work, in Crashaw, Vaughan, and Harvey. The basic structure of *The Temple* is essentially typological. As Tuve points out:

Herbert is almost as preoccupied with the relation between the Old Dispensation and the New as are the typological materials and the allegorical glosses which he so often echoes; considerations of God as Law or rigorous Justice and God as Love are thematic not haphazard in his work, and to recognize this theme is to become aware of a unity in the whole body of work which Herbert did not live to perfect but which is an aesthetic satisfaction to anyone who reads him whole. This is a book about Ecclesia, and her great Type, Synagogue, is as ever-present here as she had been in presentations of Ecclesia in other forms of symbolic Christian Art.[20]

In the typological context, the temple symbol is actually capable of more than one reference. It is, first of all, the actual historical temple of the Old Testament, the place of worship with all its furnishings. In this sense, it is a type of the Church buildings of the New Dispensation built in varying degrees on the pattern of Solomon's temple. The temple is also the Mystical Body of Christ, the Church, the people of God, the Chosen Seed of the New Testament, with its liturgical observances and feasts, its priesthood as the fulfillment of the Old Testament priesthood of Melchisedech and Aaron. Finally, the temple is the temple of the Holy Spirit, the soul of the individual Christian in its struggles, its penitence, and its love. Throughout *The Temple*, Herbert is making use of all these references, sometimes explicitly and sometimes implicitly, weaving them into one harmonious whole, with overtones and added meanings gathered from all the possible typological correspondences.

What Herbert seems to have done is to take up now one plane, now another, sometimes with an obvious reason for the shifting of the point of view, very often, as far as we can tell, without any.[21]

[19]   Lancelot Andrewes, *Works*, II, 347-438.
[20]   Tuve, *A Reading of George Herbert*, 123.
[21]   White, *Metaphysical Poets*, 159.

Most obviously, and most frequently, Herbert uses the temple as a type of his own soul,

> ... a picture of the many spiritual conflicts that have passed between God and my Soul, before I could subject mine to the will of Jesus my Master; in whose service I have now found perfect freedom.[22]

Herbert's *Temple* is therefore "the symbolic record ... of a 'typical' Christian life within the Church".[23] In an added and even deeper sense, *The Temple* is the type of the priestly vocation of Herbert in the service of God. This priestly vocation in the temple, is also the type of Herbert's vocation as poet, as seen for example, in the *Jordan* poems, and in *The Windows*.

Herbert makes good use of this temple typology in *Sion*, where he builds his poem upon the concept of the New Ecclesia, the New Temple, built in the hearts of the faithful. The poem, as Tuve points out, is "ostensibly about Solomon's temple, really about Zion, the faithful people of the Church of God — at any time".[24] Herbert speaks of the glory with which God was served, "When Solomons temple stood and flourished" (1.2):

> And now thy Architecture meets with sinne;
> For all thy frame and fabrick is within.
> (ll. 11-12)

The contrast between the type and the antitype is very clear:

> And truly brasse and stones are heavie things,
> Tombes for the dead, not temples fit for thee.
> (ll. 19-20)

It is a very simple poem, yet very rich in its implications of shadow and fulfillment.

Very closely connected with the temple typology is the Priest typology, especially that of Aaron and Melchisedech.[25] Augustine says that Aaron is "umbra et figura aeterni sacerdotis"[26] and Milton echoes this when he says that "Aaron typified a better reality".[27] In the same work Milton

---

[22] I. Walton, *Life of G. Herbert*, 314

[23] Summers, *George Herbert*, 85.

[24] Tuve, *A Reading of George Herbert*, 125.

[25] Another similar type theme is that of Isaac as a sacrificial type of Christ, though this relationship does not occur too frequently in seventeenth-century literature. The typology is based on Hebrews 11:17-19 and Galatians 3:15, 4:21-29. For the patristic tradition, see Jean Danielou, "La Typologie d'Isaac dans le christianisme primitif", *Biblica*, XXVIII (1947), 363-393.

[26] *De Civ. Dei*, 17, 6. For further references, see G. Bardy, "Melchisédech dans la tradition patristique", *Revue Biblique* (1926), 416 ff. and (1927), 24 ff.

[27] *Likeliest Means to Remove Hirelings*, Hughes edition, 860.

speaks of Melchisedech as "a type of Christ and his priesthood".[28]
Andrewes uses Melchisedech as a type of Christ with a clear indication of
the *forma perfectior* in Christ:

> ... He (Christ) is Melchisedech, King and Priest; ready to bring forth as he did
> bread and wine. (Gen. 14:18). But in another manner far than he did. The
> bread and wine Melchisedech brought forth were not his body and blood;
> Christ's are ...[29]

Melchisedech is a type of Christ because of a eucharistic correspondence.
He brings forth bread and wine, and is thus linked to Christ through the
manna in the desert and the Last Supper. Herbert uses this typological
symbolism in his poem *Peace*. In the poem, Melchisedech is a type of
Christ, Salem is a type of Jerusalem, bread is made from the twelve
stalks that grow out of Melchisedech's grave, types of the twelve tribes
and of the twelve apostles who carry the bread of Peace.[30]

As Hutchinson says in his notes, Vaughan realized that Herbert wrote of
Christ, for Melchisedech, "King of Salem, which is, King of Peace" (Heb. 7:2)
prefigured Christ. Not only is this true, but the centuries which had made this
one of the firmest of all symbolic conventions had so ecclesiasticized it that
none could be more suited to Herbert's unifying theme. Few could be unaware
that Melchisedech, the Priest-King, prefigured Christ in his character as the
Eucharist; Melchisedech's action in giving bread and wine to Abraham is the
Old Testament type of Christ's feeding of his Church, and Christ is the God
who nourishes, the priest who officiates, the King, and the sacrifice (the Body,
Bread, spiritual food) which is eaten. This is a Holy Communion Poem, but it
is also a poem of the Apostles' mission, and of *corpus christi* as the Bread but
simultaneously as that "mystical Body" of Christ of whom men may become
"very members incorporate."[31]

The full context of the temple typology, as has been seen, includes what
may be called liturgical typology.[32] This is the use of ceremonies and
rites of the Old Testament Worship in the Temple as historical and
meaningful ceremonies in themselves, but also as adumbrations of greater
and more meaningful ceremonies to come. Thus, the bloody sacrifices of
sheep and goats in the Old Testament Mosaic Law were types of the

---

[28]   *Likeliest Means* ..., 861.
[29]   *Nativity Sermons*, 165. See also p. 291.
[30]   Tuve, *A Reading of George Herbert*, 71-72. Also see Summers, *George Herbert*, 176.
[31]   Tuve, *A Reading of George Herbert*, 161-162. In addition to the Melchisedech typology, Herbert makes great use of Aaron as a type of Christ, and as a type of his own
vocation as priest-poet. A fuller development of this theme would provide a very
fruitful field for investigation into Herbert's use of typology. The relationship is merely
indicated here, but again, there is room for much further study of the Priest-Poet
relationship in seventeenth-century literature.
[32]   See the discussion of Liturgical types in the Exodus in Chapter VIII.

sacrifice of the New Testament. This sort of Liturgical type is used in Vaughan's *Faith*:

> The Law, and Ceremonies made
> A glorious night,
> Where Stars, and Clouds, both light, and shade
> Had equal right;
> But, as in nature, when the day
> Breaks, night adjourns,
> Stars shut up shop, mists pack away,
> And the Moon mourns;
> So when the Sun of righteousness
> Did once appear,
> That scene was chang'd, and a new dresse
> Left for us here;
> Veiles became useless, Altars fel,
> Fires smoking die;
> And all that sacred pomp, and shel
> Of things did flie;
> Then did he shine forth, whose sad fall,
> And bitter flights
> Were figur'd in those mystical
> And Cloudie Rights ...
> (ll. 13-32)

Also closely connected with the notion of temple typology is the use of what might be called political typology in the literature of the seventeenth century. Professor Mazzeo has analyzed one example of this sort of political type in his article on "Cromwell as Davidic King" in the poems of Andrew Marvell.[33] Dante uses the same sort of typology in *De Monarchia*, and there are many other examples of it in seventeenth-century literature. This sort of typology, however, is only indirectly Christic; the typological relationship is established between two historical personages in the Old and New Testament, for example between Cromwell and David. But in this correspondence, it is actually David, the Old Testament figure, who is the antitype, the *forma perfectior*, and Cromwell looks back to David rather than forward to a greater antitype who follows. There is no direct reference to Christ, except insofar as David himself is a type of Christ as King. To this extent, this sort of political type is not a strict typological relationship as has been defined above; it is rather analogically typological, and the danger is that it can slip over into allegory or mere biblical allusion.

This is certainly the case in the use of mythical figures as a sort of

---

[33]   J. A. Mazzeo, ed., *Reason and the Imagination* (New York: Columbia University Press, 1962), 29-55.

quasi-typology. Mythical typology abandons the historical reality of the Old Testament types completely, and uses the persons, events, institutions of Pagan mythology as types and foreshadowings of the New Testament events. But since the essential reality of the type is destroyed, so is the basic notion of typology. As Summers points out, "The idea of the types could be extended to profane literature and could partially sanctify it",[34] but such use of typology is essentially analogical.

As time went on, figural interpretation became a kind of second nature to Christian intellectuals, and pagan material came to be figurally interpreted. The Sibyl, Virgil, the Grail story, the legend of the Seven Sleepers, Charlemagne and others were all conceived at least in partially figural terms. The most striking and familiar application of this technique to secular materials is Dante's *De Monarchia* where not only is there posited a correspondence between secular and sacred history but the great characters of Roman history are given some of that exemplary and figural character they will have in such a striking degree in the *Divine Comedy*.[35]

This mythical typology had its roots in the Fathers who often looked upon Apollo, Prometheus, Hercules and other mythical figures as types of Christ.[36]

Milton makes extensive use of this mythical typology throughout his work. In the *Nativity Ode*, for example, Christ is a more perfect Pan (ll. 88), and in the *Passion*, Christ is Hercules (l. 13). In *Paradise Regained*, Milton establishes a relationship between the struggle of Christ and Satan, and the conflict of Hercules and Antaeus (*P.R.* 4:563-571). In Stanza 7 of *Christ's Triumph over Death*, Giles Fletcher says:

> Who doth not see drown'd in Deucalion's name,
> (When earth his men, and sea had lost his shore)
> Old Noah; and in Nisus look, the fame
> Of Samson yet alive; and long before
> In Phaethons, mine own fall I deplore,
> But he that conquer'd hell, to fetch againe
> His virgin widowe, by a serpent slaine,
> Another Orpheus was then dreaming poets feigne.

This has all the machinery, but it is not strict typology, because the reality of the type is an assumed fact. At this point biblical typology, as used in the literary works of any period, becomes less and less typological, and begins to assume the trappings of increasingly subjective allegory and mythical metaphor.

---

[34]   Joseph Summers, "Herbert's Form", 1061.
[35]   Joseph A. Mazzeo, *Medieval Cultural Tradition in Dante's Comedy*, 179.
[36]   See for example, Jacobus Bonus, *De Vita et Gestis Christi ... atque Herculis labores et gesta in Christi Figuram*, Rome, 1526.

There can be little doubt of either the relevance or prevalence of the typological world view in the literature of the seventeenth century. The typological themes here discussed are just a few of the many examples of biblical typology used by the poets and literary men of the century. It was an age that still thought much of "Divine Poems" and religious themes, and most of the writers were as deeply versed in theology as they were in literature. The Bible was still read as a meaningful record of God's providential care and of the relevance of the divine and the eternal at every moment of temporal history. The biblical story was structured on an essentially typological basis, and these typological concepts were inevitably reflected in the literature of an age that looked so frequently and so easily to the Bible and the traditions of the Fathers for meaning and instruction in all their contemporary problems. Thus it was that Donne could speak so easily of his own Exodus from the Egypt of sin, and Herbert could structure a whole volume on the temple typology of Paul and the Fathers.

The literary men of the seventeenth century were not necessarily professional theologians, however. They do not speak explicitly in terms of reality of type and antitype, metaphysical correspondence, fulfillment, recapitulation, Christic correspondence and divine relevance, but all these elements are implicit in their use of genuine typological images. These elements are so much a part of their point of view and so commonly known and accepted by their readers that they do not need explication. The typological interpretation of the Bible is the common presupposition of almost every one of the literary men of the seventeenth century, and even where it does not form the basic imagery of any literary work, it adds a deeper meaning to almost every one of the poems written on biblical themes. An understanding of the theological and scriptural basis of typology leads inevitably to a more profound understanding and appreciation of much of the poetry and prose work of the seventeenth century.

Markus' comments about the New Testament writers are equally applicable to the writers of the seventeenth century:

Chief among the things which stand behind the New Testament writers is, of course, the Old Testament, which shaped their whole mental world and literary climate. Though its relevance is pervasive, discretion is required; its omnipresence gives no support for a wholesale search for allusions to particular Old Testament passages or images in every New Testament text ... In clothing the New Testament in Old Testament imagery and weaving narratives in patterns borrowed from the Old Testament, the writers are presenting the events they describe in terms of their significance in God's plan for the redemption of men ... The various and often interweaving patterns which hinge on these images have always been a rich source for discerning further correspondence and relations.[37]

The richness of much of seventeenth-century literature is a richness that is borrowed from the typological structure and images of the richest of all books, the Bible. For, as Markus points out, "the typology of anticipation and fulfillment is the basic category of a Christian understanding of history".[38]

[37]   Markus, "Presuppositions of the Typological Approach to Scripture", 79.
[38]   Markus, 85.

TYPOLOGY AND THE FOURFOLD SENSE OF SCRIPTURE

The analysis of the various senses of scripture is a complicated problem and it is often difficult, if not impossible, to correlate all the various terms in use among scripture scholars down through the history of biblical exegesis. The ambiguity in the term allegory in Paul, Origen, and some of the earlier Fathers has already been indicated. The question is complicated even further in more recent studies of scripture where authors distinguish the literal, the figurative, and typological senses, as well as the consequent sense, the *sensus plenior*, the accommodated sense and the anagogic, tropological, moral and ethical senses.[1] A full treatment of all these senses is far beyond the scope of the present study. But since the fourfold interpretation of scripture is so prevalent in the Middle Ages and in the Renaissance, the relationship between this fourfold sense of scripture and the typological sense as it has been proposed in the present study, should be briefly indicated.

The traditional fourfold interpretation of scripture is expressed in the distich from Nicholas of Lyra:

> Littera gesta docet, quid credas allegoria;
> Moralis quid agas, quo tendas anagogia.[2]

Henri de Lubac has discussed this fourfold interpretation and the understanding of this distich in the Middle Ages in his monumental work,[3] and there is little that need be added to his comments there. The classical literary interpretation of this fourfold interpretation of scripture is contained in Dante's letter to Can Grande della Scala:

For the clarity of what is to be said, one must realize that the meaning of the work is not simple, but is rather to be called polysemous, that is, having many

---

[1] For one example of an attempt to correlate the various terminologies, see X. Patrizi, *Institutio de Interpretatione Librorum Bibliorum* (Rome, 1876) and also Coppens, *Les Harmonies des deux Testaments*, 13, 71 and *passim*.
[2] *PL* 113:28.
[3] *Exégèse Médiévale: Les quatre sens de l'Écriture* (Paris, 1959).

meanings. The first meaning is the one obtained through the letter; the second
is the one obtained through the things signified by the letter. The first is called
literal, the second allegorical or moral or anagogical. In order that this manner
of treatment may appear more clearly, it may be applied to the following
verses: "When Israel went out of Egypt, the house of Jacob from a people of
strange language, Judah was his sanctuary and Israel his dominion." (Psalm
114:1-2). For if we look to the letter alone, the departure of the children of
Israel from Egypt in the time of Moses is indicated to us; if to the allegory,
our redemption accomplished by Christ is indicated to us; if to the moral
sense, the conversion of the soul from the woe and misery of sin to a state of
grace is indicated to us; if to the analogical sense, the departure of the conse-
crated soul from the slavery of this corruption to the liberty of eternal glory is
indicated. And though these mystic senses may be called by various names,
they can all generally be spoken of as allegorical, since they are diverse from
the literal or historical. For allegory is derived from *alleon* in Greek, which
in Latin appears as *alienum* or diverse.[4]

It is clear from Dante's explanation of the Exodus imagery that the
typological interpretation as it has been expressed in the present work,
actually overlaps the fourfold interpretation of scripture. Each one of the
three figurative, or mystic, allegorical senses can be typological, though
the three mystic senses are far from being synonomous with typological
concepts.

The literal interpretation is the basis of all typology, of course, and it is
the essential constituent of the phenomenal reality of both the type and
the antitype. The allegorical or figurative sense is often identical with the
typological view, and in Dante's interpretation of Psalm 114, the image
actually is typological. The anagogical sense can also be typological.
But this is most often an extended sense of typology, since the difficulty
is always present of determining the phenomenal reality of the antitype
at the eschaton. Markus points out that the anagogical antitype derives
from a "wrench in the biblical time-scheme".

The Old Testament as a whole, and particular passages of it in special ways,
foretold, promised, and prefigured the Messiah who was to come "in the last
times." What was pointed to had come to pass — God had revealed his ways
with men in Christ — and yet, it had still to come; the salvation he brought
had still to be clinched, and shown forth among men at his second coming in
glory. Hence where the Old Testament points forward to its fulfillment, it has
a double reference: it may point either to the Incarnation and its events, or the
final consummation of earthly history, or to both. We have already discussed
the manner in which it prefigures the events of the New Testament narrative.
The New Testament itself, however, is witness that the Old Testament was

[4]   Alan H. Gilbert, *Literary Criticism: Plato to Dryden* (New York: American Book
Company, 1940), 202-203.

taken as pointing beyond the fulfillment already realized to the ἔσχατον. Jerusalem, the sanctuary of Israel, foreshadows at once Christ and his Body, the Church *in via* and the heavenly church united to her Lord in glory. This further reference to the ἔσχατον is what the medieval tradition knew as the "anagogical" interpretation; and however limited the scope for "anagogical" interpretation may be, in view of the reserve of the scriptural indications, a place for it had to be safeguarded if the great outlines of the economy of redemption with its time-scheme was to remain at the foundation of all "spiritual" exegesis.[5]

Typology is open to moral interpretation as well, though in most cases, the moral sense departs from the reality of events and becomes involved in rather subjective allegory. In practice, the moral sense is most often little more than a homiletic, allegorical use of the biblical text for the purposes of moral exhortation, and is practically identical with the accommodated sense of scripture. This danger of subjective allegory is actually present in all of the three mystic senses of the fourfold interpretation of scripture. They are often allegorical, rather than typological. In determining genuine typology in any particular case — whether it be allegorical, moral or anagogical — the characteristics of type and antitype which have been indicated in the first part of the present study must be rigidly applied.[6]

---

[5] Markus, "Presuppositions of the Typological Approach to Scripture", pp. 83-84.
[6] Erich Auerbach has discussed the relationship of the typological interpretation of Scripture to the medieval four senses of Scripture. Although he prefers to speak of typology as "figural interpretation" his views in that essay are substantially those as outlined in this Appendix.

BIBLIOGRAPHY

Abbott, John, *Jesus Prefigured: Or a Poem of the Holy Name of Jesus* (Antwerp, 1623).
Alexander, Sir William, *Doomes-Day, or the Great Day of the Lord's Judgment*, 1614, edited by L. E. Kastner and H. B. Charlton (= *Scottish Text Society*, Vol. XXIV, n.s.) (Edinburgh, 1929).
Allen, Don Cameron, "John Donne Sets His Text", *ELH*, X (1934), 208-229.
—, "John Donne's 'Paradise and Calvarie'", *Modern Language Notes*, LX (1945).
—, *The Legend of Noah: Renaissance Rationalism in Art, Science and Letters* (Urbana, Illinois: University of Illinois Press, 1949).
—, "Marvell's 'Nymph'", *ELH*, XXIII (1956), 93-111.
Andrewes, Lancelot, *Seven Sermons on the wonderful combat for God's glory and man's salvation between Christ and Satan*, 1592. Reprinted in *Ninety-Six Sermons*, edited by John Parkinson (Oxford, 1841-1843).
—, *Sermons on the Nativity* (Grand Rapids, Michigan: Baker Book House, 1955).
—, *The Private Devotions*, edited and with an introduction by Thomas S. Kepler (Cleveland-New York: World Publishing Company, 1956).
Armendarez, Luis M., S.J., *El Nuevo Moises Dinamica Cristocentica en la Tipologia de Cirilo Alejandrino* (= *Estudios Oniensis*, Series 3) (Madrid: Ediciones Fax, 1962).
Atkins, J. W. H., *English Literary Criticism: The Renascence* (London: Methuen, 1947).
Aubert, R., "Discussions récentes autour de la Théologie de l'Histoire", *Collectanea Mechliniensia*, XXXIII (n.s. XVIII) (1948), 129-149.
Auerbach, Erich, "Figura", *Archivum Romanicum*, XXII (1938), 436-489. The same article is reprinted with minor changes in *Neue Dantestudien* (Istanbul, 1944). There is an English translation of the same article by Ralph Manheim in *Scenes From the Drama of European Literature*. See the entry below.
—, "Typological Symbolism in Medieval Literature", *Yale French Studies*, IX (1952), 3-10.
—, *Mimesis*, translated by Willard Trask (Princeton: Princeton University Press, 1953).
—, *Typologische Motive in der Mittelalterlichen Literatur* (Krefeld: Scherpe-Verlag, 1953).
—, "Figurative Texts Illustrating Certain Passages of Dante's Commedia", *Speculum*, XXI (1956), 474-489.
—, *Scenes From the Drama of European Literature* (New York: Meridian Books, 1959).
—, *Introduction to Romance Language and Literature*, translated by Guy Daniels (New York: Capricorn Books, 1961).
Bacon, Francis, *The Advancement of Learning*, edited by William Aldis Wright (Oxford, 1900). There is also an "Everyman Edition" (London: J. M. Dent and Sons, 1930). Also an edition by Richard Foster Jones (New York: Odyssey Press, 1937).
Bainton, Roland H., "The Bible in the Reformation", *The Cambridge History of the Bible: The West From the Reformation to the Present Day*, edited by S. L. Greenslade (Cambridge: Cambridge University Press, 1963), 1-37.

Baldwin, Edward C., "Some Extra-Biblical Semitic Influences on Milton's Story of the Fall of Man", *JEGP*, XXVIII (1929), 366-401.

von Balthasar, Hans Ur, *A Theology of History* (New York: Sheed and Ward, 1963).

Bardy, G., "Melchisédech dans la tradition patristique", *Revue Biblique* (1926), 416 ff. and (1927), 24 ff.

—, "L'exégèse patristique", *Initiation Biblique*, edited by A. Robert and A. Tricot, troisième édition réfondue (Paris: Desclée et Cie, 1954), 455-466.

Barr, James, *Biblical Words for Time* (Naperville, Illinois: Alec R. Allenson, Inc., 1962).

—, *Old and New In Interpretation* (London: SCM Press, Ltd,. 1966).

Beaumont, Joseph, *The Minor Poems*, edited by E. Robinson (New York, 1914).

Beaupère, René, O.P., "La Bible, Source de l'Imaginaire Chretien", *La Vie Spirituelle*, No. 472 (Mai, 1961), 496-505.

Berdyaev, Nicolas, *The Meaning of History* (New York: Charles Scribner's Sons, 1936).

Bewley, M., "Religious Cynicism in Donne's Poetry", *Kenyon Review*, XIV (1952), 619-646.

Blaser, Peter, M.S.C., "St. Paul's Use of the Old Testament", *Theological Quarterly*, CXXXIII (1952), 152-169.

Boman, Thorlief, *Hebrew Thought Compared with Greek*, translated by Jules Moreau (Philadelphia: Westminster Press, 1960).

Bonsirven, Joseph, S.J., "Saint Paul et l'ancien Testament", *Nouvelle Revue Theologique*, LXV (1938), 129-147.

—, "L'exégèse Juive", *Initiation Biblique*, edited by A. Robert and A. Tricot (Paris: Desclée et Cie, 1954), 450-455.

—, *Exégèse rabbinique et exégèse paulinienne* (Paris: Beauchesne, 1957).

Bonus, Jacobus, *De Vita et Gestis Christi ... atque Herculis labores et Gesta in Christi Figuram* (Rome, 1526).

Bottrall, Margaret, *George Herbert* (London: John Murray, 1954).

Bowers, Fredson, "Henry Vaughan's Multiple Time Scheme", *Modern Language Quarterly*, XXIII (1962), 291-296.

Bredvold, Louis I., *The Intellectual Milieu of John Dryden* (Ann Arbor: University of Michigan Press, 1959).

Broadbent, J. B., *Some Graver Subject* (New York: Barnes and Noble, 1960).

Brown, Raymond E., S.S., "The History and Development of the Theory of a *Sensus Plenior*", *The Catholic Biblical Quarterly*, XV (1953), 141-162.

—, *The Sensus Plenior in Sacred Scripture* (Baltimore: St. Mary's University Press, 1955).

—, "The *Sensus Plenior* in the Last Ten Years", *The Catholic Biblical Quarterly*, XXV (1963), 262-285.

—, "Hermeneutics", *The Jerome Biblical Commentary*, edited by Raymond E. Brown, S.S. *et al.* (Englewood Cliffs, N.J.: Prentice-Hall, Inc., 1968), 605-623.

Browne, Sir Thomas, *Religio Medici* (New York: E. P. Dutton, 1951).

Brunner, Emil, "The Christian Sense of Time", *Cross Currents*, I (1950), 25-33. Translated by Joseph E. Cunneen from the original in *Dieu Vivant*, No. 14, 15-30.

Bultmann, D. Rudolf., *History and Eschatology* (Edinburgh: The University Press, 1957).

Burghardt, Walter, J., S.J., "Theotokos: The Mother of God", *The Mystery of the Woman*, edited by Edward D. O'Connor, C.S.C. (Notre Dame, Indiana: University of Notre Dame Press, 1956), 5-30. The same article is also reprinted in *The Idea of Catholicism*, edited by Walter J. Burghardt, S.J. and William F. Lynch, S.J. (New York: Greenwich Edition of Meridian Books, 1960), 166-183.

—, "On Early Christian Exegesis", *Theological Studies*, XI (1950), 78-116.

Burlin, Robert B., *The Old English Advent: A Typological Commentary* (New York: Yale University Press, 1968).

Bush, Douglas, *Paradise Lost In Our Time* (New York, 1945).
—, *English Literature in the Earlier Seventeenth Century: 1600-1660*, 2nd. ed. revised (Oxford: Clarendon Press, 1962).
Butterfield, H., *Christianity and History* (New York: Charles Scribner's Sons, 1950).
The Cambridge History of the Bible: The West from the Reformation to the Present Day, edited by S. L. Greenslade (Cambridge: Cambridge University Press, 1963).
Case, Shirley Jackson, *The Christian Philosophy of History* (Chicago: University of Chicago Press, 1943).
Charity, A. C., *Events and their Afterlife* (Cambridge: Cambridge University Press, 1966).
Charlier, Dom Celestin, "La Lecture sapientelle de la Bible", *MD*, XII (1947), 31ff.
—, *The Christian Approach to the Bible*, translated by Robert J. Richards and Brendan Peters (Westminster, Maryland: The Newman Press, 1958).
—, "Méthode historique et lecture spirituelle des Écritures", *Bible et Vie Chrétienne*, XVIII (1957). There is a translation by John P. McCall in William F. Lynch, *Christ and Apollo* (New York: Sheed and Ward, 1960).
Clark, Donald Leman, *John Milton at St. Paul's School* (New York: Columbia University Press, 1948).
Clark, W. Norris, S.J., "Bibliography on Theology and History", *News* of the Institute for Religious and Social Studies Fellowship, 3600 Broadway, New York 27, New York (November, 1953).
Coffin, Charles Monroe, *John Donne and the New Philosophy* (New York, 1938).
Colie, R. L., "Some Paradoxes in the Language of Things", *Reason and the Imagination*, edited by Joseph A. Mazzeo (New York: Columbia University Press, 1962), 93-128.
Common Prayer, The Book of, and Administrations of the Sacraments and Other Rites and Ceremonies of the Church of England, London, 1559. Edited for the Parker Society by Rev. William Keating Clay (Cambridge: At the University Press, 1847).
Congar, Yves, *Christ, Our Lady and the Church* (Westminster, Maryland: The Newman Press, 1951).
—, "Marie et l'Église dans la pensée patristique", *Revue des Sciences Philosophiques et Théologiques*, XXXVIII (1954), 3-38.
Conklin, George N., *Biblical Criticism and Heresy in Milton* (New York: King's Crown Press, Columbia University, 1949).
Cope, Gilbert, *Symbolism in the Bible and the Church* (London: SCM Press, Ltd., 1959).
Coppens, Joseph, *Les Harmonies des deux Testaments*, nouvelle édition révue et augmentée (Tournai-Paris: Casterman, 1949).
Courtade, Gaston, "Le sens de l'histoire dans l'Écriture et la classification usuelle des sens scripturaires", *Recherches de Science Religieuse*, XXXVI (1949).
Crashaw, Richard, *The Poems*, edited by L. C. Martin (Oxford: At the Clarendon Press, 1957).
Cullman, Oscar, *Temps et histoire dans le Christianisme primitif* (Neuchâtel et Paris: Imprimerie Delachaux et Niestle, 1947).
—, *Christ and Time: The Primitive Christian Conception of Time and History*, translated by Floyd V. Filson (Philadelphia: Westminster Press, 1950).
Curtius, Ernest Robert, *European Literature and the Latin Middle Ages*, translated by Williard R. Trask (New York: Pantheon Books, Inc., 1953).
Cushman, Robert E., "Greek and Christian Views of Time", *The Journal of Religion*, XXXIII (1953), 254-265.
Danielou, Jean, "Traversée de la Mer Rouge et baptême aux premiers siècles", *Recherches de Science Religieuse*, XXXIII (1946), 402-430.
—, "Déluge, baptême, jugement", *Dieu Vivant*, VIII (1947). 97-112.
—, "Le symbolisme du baptême", *Dieu Vivant*, I (1947).

—, "La typologie d'Isaac dans le christianisme primitif", *Biblica*, XXVIII (1947), 363-393.

—, "Les divers sens de l'Écriture dans la tradition primitive", *Ephemerides Theologicae Lovanienses*, XXIV (1948), 119-126.

—, "The Conception of History in the Christian Tradition", *The Journal of Religion*, XXX (1950), 171-179.

—, *Sacramentum Futuri: Études sur les origines de la typologie biblique* (Paris: Beauchesne et ses Fils, 1950) (English translation entitled *From Shadows to Reality*).

—, "A Dialogue with Time", *Cross Currents*, I (1951), 78-90. Translated by Bernard Gilligan from the original in *Études*, October, 1947.

—, *Origen*, translated by Walter Mitchell (New York: Sheed and Ward, 1955).

—, *The Lord of History*, translated by Nigel Abercrombie (London: Longmans, 1958).

—, *From Shadows to Reality: Studies in the Biblical Typology of the Fathers*, translated by Dom Wulfstan Hibbard (Westminster, Maryland: Newman Press, 1960).

Davies, Horton, *The Worship of the English Puritans* (London: Dacre Press, 1948).

Delporte, Lucien, "Les principes de la typologie biblique et les élements figuratifs du sacrifice de l'expiation (Lev. 16)", *Ephemerides Theologicae Lovanienses* (1926), 306-327.

Dentan, Robert C., "Typology — Its Use and Abuse", *Anglican Theological Review*, XXXIV (1952), 210-217.

Dodd, C. H., *According to the Scriptures: The Sub-Structure of New Testament Theology* (New York: Charles Scribner's Sons, 1953).

Donne, John, *Essays in Divinity*, edited by Evelyn M. Simpson (Oxford: Clarendon Press, 1952).

—, *The Divine Poems*, edited by Helen Gardner (Oxford: Clarendon Press, 1952).

—, *The Sermons*, edited, with Introduction and Critical Apparatus by George R. Potter and Evelyn M. Simpson, 10 vols. (Berkeley and Los Angeles: University of California Press, 1953).

—, *Poetical Works*, edited by Herbert J. Grierson, 2 vols. (Oxford: University Press, 1958).

—, *The Sermons*, selected and with an introduction by Theodore H. Gill (New York: Meridian Books, Inc., 1958).

—, *Devotions Upon Emergent Occasions* together with *Death's Duell* (Ann Arbor: University of Michigan Press, 1959).

—, *The Anniversaries*, edited by Frank Manley (Baltimore: John Hopkins Press, 1963).

Donohue, Charles, "Patristic Exegesis: Summation", *Critical Approaches to Medieval Literature*, edited by Dorothy Bethurum (New York: Columbia University Press, 1960).

Doughty, W. L., *Studies in Religious Poetry* (1947).

Drayton, Michael, *Moses: His Birth and Miracles* (1604).

Dubarle, A. M., "Le sens spirituel de l'Écriture", *Revue SR*, XXXI (1947).

Durr, R. A., *On the Mystical Poetry of Henry Vaughan* (Cambridge: Harvard University Press, 1962).

Edsman, C. M., "Gammal och ny typologish tolkning av G.T.", *Svensk exegetisk arsbok* (1947), 85-109.

Eichrodt, Walther, "Ist die typologische Exegese sachgemässe Exegese?", *Probleme alttestamentlicher Hermeneutik*, edited by Claus Westermann (Munich Chr. Kaiser Verlag, 1960).

Ellis, Edward Earle, *Paul's Use of the Old Testament* (Edinburgh: Oliver and Boyd, 1957).

Empson, William, *English Pastoral Poetry* (New York: Norton, 1938).

—, "Marvell's Garden", *Some Versions of Pastoral* (New York: New Directions, 1960).

—, *Milton's God* (New York: New Directions, 1961).

—, *Seven Types of Ambiguity* (New York: Meridian Books, 1963).

Fitzmyer, Joseph A., S.J., "The Use of Explicit Old Testament Quotations in Qumran Literature and in the New Testament", *New Testament Studies*, VII (1960-1961), 298-333.

Fletcher, Giles, *Christ's Victorie. Poetical Works of Giles Fletcher and Phineas Fletcher*, edited by Frederick S. Boas, 2 vols. (Cambridge: University Press, 1908).

Fletcher, Harris Francis, *Milton's Semitic Studies and Some Manifestations of Them in His Poetry* (Chicago: University of Chicago Press, 1926).

—, *The Use of the Bible in Milton's Prose* (Urbana: University of Illinois Press, 1929).

—, *Milton's Rabbinical Readings* (Urbana: University of Illinois Press, 1930).

—, *The Intellectual Development of John Milton*, 2 vols. (Urbana: University of Illinois Press, 1956, 1961).

Frye, Northrop, "The Typology of Paradise Regained", *MP*, LIII (1956), 227-238.

Frye, Northrop, L. C. Knight, *et al.*, eds., *Myth and Symbol* (Lincoln, Nebraska: University of Nebraska Press).

Gardner, Helen, *The Limits of Literary Criticism: Reflections on the Interpretation of Poetry and Scripture* (London: Oxford University Press, 1956).

—, ed., *The Metaphysical Poets* (Penguin Books, 1957).

Garner, Ross, *Henry Vaughan: Experience and the Tradition* (Chicago: University of Chicago Press, 1959).

Gilbert, Alan H., *Literary Criticism: Plato to Dryden* (New York: American Book Company, 1940).

Gill, Alexander, *Sacred Philosophy of Holy Scripture* (1635).

Gilson, Etienne, *The Spirit of Medieval Philosophy*, translated by A. H. C. Downes (New York: Charles Scribner's Sons, 1940).

Goodman, Godfrey, *The Fall of man, or the Corruption of Nature Proved by the Light of Natural Reason* (1616).

Goppelt, Leonhard, *Typos: Die Typologische Deutung des alten Testaments im Neuen* (Gutersich, 1939).

Greenslade, S. L., ed., *The Cambridge History of the Bible: The West from the Reformation to the Present Day* (Cambridge: Cambridge University Press, 1963).

Gribement, J., "Le lien des deux testaments selon la théologie de Saint Thomas: Notes sur le sens spirituel et implicite des Saintes Écritures", *Ephemerides Theologicae Lovanienses*, XXII (1946), 70-89.

—, "Sens plenier, sens typique, et sens litteral", *Problème et Méthode d'Exégèse Théologique*.

Grisbrooke, W. Jardine, ed., *Anglican Liturgies of the Seventeenth and Eighteenth Centuries* (London: SPCK, 1958).

Guild, William, *Moses Unveiled: or those figures which served unto the patterne and shadow of heavenly things, pointing out the Messiah, Christ Jesus, briefly explained.* Edited for the Christian Treasury by Rev. T. S. Wemes (London: Henry G. Bohm, 1849).

Guillet, J., "La thème de la marche au désert dans l'Ancien et le Nouveau Testament", *Recherches de Science Religieuse*, XXXVI (1949), 164ff.

Hakewill, George, *An Apologie for the Power and Providence of God in the Government of the World* (1627).

Haller, William, "The Tragedy of God's Englishman", *Reason and the Imagination*, edited by Joseph A. Mazzeo (New York: Columbia University Press, 1962).

Hanford, James Holly, "The Temptation Motive in Milton", *SP*, XV (1918), 176-194.

—, *Studies in Shakespeare, Milton and Donne* (= *University of Michigan Publications in Language and Literature*, I) (New York, 1925).

Hanson, Richard P. C., "Moses in the Typology of St. Paul", *Theology*, XLVIII (1945), 174-177.

—, *Allegory and Event: A Study of the Sources and Significance of Origen's Interpretation of Scripture* (Richmond, Virginia: John Knox Press, 1959).

Harris, Victor, *All Coherence Gone* (Chicago, 1949).

Harrison, J. S., *Platonism in English Poetry of the Sixteenth and Seventeenth Century* (New York, 1903).

Hart, Jeffrey, "*Paradise Lost* and Order", *College English*, XXV (1964), 576-582.

Harvey, Christopher, *Synagogue: or the Shadow of the Temple*, 1640.

Haynes, Thomas, *The General View of Scripture* (London, 1640).

Hazelton, Roger, "Time, Eternity, and History", *The Journal of Religion*, XXX (1950), 1-12.

Hebert, A. C., *The Authority of the Old Testament* (London: Faber and Faber, Ltd., 1947).

Henry, Paul, S.J., "The Christian Philosophy of History", *Theological Studies*, XIII (1952), 419-432.

Herbert, George, *The Works*, edited by F. E. Hutchinson (Oxford: Clarendon Press, 1959).

Herrick, Robert, *Poetical Works*, edited by L. C. Martin (Oxford: Clarendon Press, 1956).

Holborn, Hajo, "Greek and Modern Concepts of History", *Journal of the History of Ideas*, X (1949), 3-13.

Hook, Sidney, ed., *Religious Experience and Truth* (New York: New York University Press).

Hunter, William B., "Milton on the Incarnation", *Journal of the History of Ideas*, XXI (1960), 349-369.

Hutchinson, F. E., *Henry Vaughan: A Life and Interpretation* (Oxford: Clarendon Press, 1947).

Hyman, L. W., "Marvell's Garden", *ELH*, XXV (1958), 13-22.

Initiation Biblique: Introduction à l'étude des Saintes Ecritures, edited by A. Robert and A. Tricot, troisième edition refondue (Paris: Desclée et Cie, 1954).

Jones, R. F., *Ancients and Moderns* (St. Louis, 1936).

Jonson, Ben, "Conversations with Drummond", *The Works*, edited by C. H. Herford and P. Simpson (Oxford: Clarendon Press, 1947).

—, *The Poems*, edited by George Burke Johnston (London: Routledge and Kegan Paul, Ltd., 1954).

Kehoe, R., "The Spiritual Sense of Scripture", *Blackfriars* (1947), 246-251.

Kelley, Maurice, *This Great Argument: A Study of Milton's De Doctrine Christiana As a Gloss Upon Paradise Lost* (Princeton: Princeton University Press, 1941).

—, "Milton's Debt to Wollebius' *Compendium Theologiae Christianae*", *PMLA*, L (1950).

Kermode, Frank, "The Argument of Marvell's Garden", *Essays in Criticism*, II (1952).

Kierkegaard, Søren, *Training in Christianity*, translated by Walter Lowrie (Oxford, 1941).

Krouse, F. Michael, *Milton's Samson and the Christian Tradition* (Princeton: Princeton University Press, 1949).

Kurth, Burton O., *Milton and Christian Heroism* (Berkeley and Los Angeles: University of California Press, 1959).

Lampe, G. W. H., "The Reasonableness of Typology", *Essays on Typology*; *Studies in Biblical Theology* (Naperville, Illinois: Alec R. Allenson, Inc., 1957).

a Lapide, Cornelius, *Commentarius in Joshue, Judicum et Ruth* (Antwerp, 1664).

Latourette, Kenneth Scott, "The Christian Understanding of History", *The American Historical Review*, LIV (1949), 259-276.

Lawry, Jon. S., "Reading *Paradise Lost*", *College English*, XXV (1964), 582-586.

Lawson, John, *The Biblical Theology of Saint Irenaeus* (London: Epworth Press, 1948).

Leah, Jonas, *The Divine Science: Aesthetic of Some Representative Seventeenth-Century English Poets* (New York, 1940).

Lederer, J., "John Donne and Emblematic Practice", *RES*, XXII (1946), 182-200.

Lestringant, Pierre, *Essai sur l'unité de la Révélation biblique* (Paris: Éditions "Je Sers", 1944).

Lewalski, Barbara K., "Structure and Symbolism of Vision in Michael's Prophecy, *PL* XI-XII", *PQ*, XLII (1963), 25-35.

Lewis, C. S., *A Preface to Paradise Lost* (London, 1943).

Lightfoot, John, *A Harmony of the Gospels*, 1654. Reprinted in *Works*, edited by John Rogers Pitman, 13 vols. (London, 1822-1825).

Loughran, Charles P., "Theology and History: A Bibliography", *Thought*, XXIX (1954), 101-115.

Lowith, Karl, *Meaning in History* (Chicago: University of Chicago Press, 1949).

de Lubac, Henri, "'Typologie' et 'Allegorie'", *Recherches de Science Religieuse*, XXXIV (1947), 180-226.

—, *Histoire et Esprit: L'Intelligence de L'Écriture d'après Origène* (Paris: Aubier, 1950).

—, *Catholicism*, translated by Lancelot C. Sheppard (New York: Sheed and Ward, 1958).

—, *Exégèse médiévale: Les quatre sens de l'Écriture*, 4 vols. (Paris: Éditions Montaigne, 1959-1964).

Lundberg, Per Ivan, *La typologie baptismale dans l'ancienne église* (Leipzig and Uppsala, 1942).

Lynch, William F., S.J., "Adventure in Order", *Thought*, XXVI (1951), 33-49.

—, "Theology and the Imagination", *Thought*, XXIX (1954-1955), 61-86, 529-554 and XXX (1955), 18-36.

—, *Christ and Apollo* (New York: Sheed and Ward, 1960). There is also a Mentor-Omega edition (New York: New American Library, 1960).

Maas, A. J., S.J., *Christ in Type and Prophecy* (New York: Benziger, 1893).

MacCallum, H. R., "Milton and Figurative Interpretation of the Bible", *University of Toronto Quarterly*, XXXI (1962), 397-415.

—, "Milton and Sacred History: Books XI and XII of *Paradise Lost*", *Essays in English Literature From the Renaissance to the Victorian Age*, edited by Miller MacLure and F. W. Watt (Toronto: University of Toronto Press, 1964), 149-168.

Madsen, William G., "Earth the Shadow of Heaven: Typological Symbolism in *Paradise Lost*", *PMLA*, LXXV (1960), 519-526.

—, *From Shadowy Types to Truth: Studies in Milton's Symbolism* (New Haven: Yale University Press, 1968).

Malevez, Leopold, S. J., "La vision chrétienne de l'histoire dans la théologie catholique", *Nouvelle Revue Theologique*, LXXI (1949), 244-264.

Markus, R. A., "Presuppositions of the Typological Approach to Scripture", *The Communication of the Gospel in New Testament Times*, edited by Austin Farrar, et al. (London: SPCK, 1961), 75-85.

Martz, Louis I., "John Donne in Meditation: The Anniversaries", *ELH*, XIV (1947), 247 ff.

—, *The Poetry of Meditation* (New Haven: Yale University Press, 1962).

—, "Henry Vaughan: The Man Within", *PMLA*, LXXVIII (1963), 40-49.

—, *The Paradise Within: Studies In Vaughan, Traherne and Milton* (New Haven: Yale University Press, 1964).

Mazzeo, Joseph Anthony, *Structure and Thought in the Paradiso* (Ithaca, New York: Cornell University Press, 1958).

—, *Medieval Cultural Tradition in Dante's Comedy* (Ithaca, New York: Cornell University Press, 1960).

—, ed., *Reason and the Imagination: Studies in the History of Ideas, 1600-1800* (New York: Columbia University Press, 1962).

—, *Renaissance and Seventeenth-Century Studies* (New York: Columbia University Press, 1964).

McKenzie, John L., S.J., *The Two Edged Sword* (Milwaukee: Bruce Publishing Co., 1956).

—, *Myths and Realities: Studies in Biblical Theology* (Milwaukee: Bruce Publishing Co., 1963).

McNally, Robert, S.J., *The Bible in the Early Middle Ages* (= *Woodstock Papers*, No. 4) (Westminster, Maryland: Newman Press, 1959).

—, "Medieval Exegesis", *Theological Studies*, XXII (1961), 445-454.

Mede, Joseph, *Discourses on Divers Texts of Scripture* (Circa 1625).

—, *Clavis Apocalypticus* (1627).

Mehl, Roger, "Philosophy of History or Theology of History", *Cross Currents*, III (1953), 162-181.

Melito of Sardis, *Homily on the Passion*, edited by Campbell Bonner (= *Studies and Documents*, edited by Kirsopp Lake and Silva Lake, Vol. XII) (London).

—, *Homélie sur la Pâque* (= *Papyrus Bodmer* XIII) (Bibliotheca Bodmeriana, 1960).

Mickelson, A. Berkeley, *Interpreting the Bible* (Grand Rapids, Michigan: Wm. B. Eardmans Publishing Company, 1963).

Milburn, R. L. P., *Early Christian Interpretation of History* (London: Adam and Charles Black, 1954).

Milton, John, *The Works*, edited by Frank A. Patterson, 18 vols. (New York: Columbia University Press, 1931-1940).

—, *Complete Poems and Major Prose*, edited by Merritt Y. Hughes (New York: Odyssey Press, 1957).

Mitchell, W. Fraser, *English Pulpit Oratory From Andrewes to Tillotson* (London: SPCK, 1932).

Mommsen, Theodor E., "St. Augustine and the Christian Idea of Progress", *Journal of the History of Ideas*, XII (1951), 346-374.

Mueller, William R., *John Donne: Preacher* (Princeton: University of Princeton Press, 1962).

Musurillo, Herbert, S.J., "History and Symbol: A Study of Form in Early Christian Literature", *Theological Studies*, XVIII (1957), 357-386.

—, "Shadow and Reality: Thoughts on the Problem of Typology", *Theological Studies*, XXII (1961), 455-460.

—, *Symbol and Myth in Ancient Poetry* (New York: Fordham University Press, 1961).

—, "Symbolism and Kerygmatic Theology", *Thought*, XXXVI (1961), 59-80.

—, *Symbolism and the Christian Imagination* (Baltimore: Helicon Press, 1962).

Nelson, Lowry Jr., *Baroque Lyric Poetry* (New Haven: Yale University Press, 1961).

Nicolson, Marjorie Hope, *The Breaking of the Circle*, revised edition (New York: Columbia University Press, 1960).

—, ed., *Milton: Poems and Selected Prose* (New York: Bantam Books, 1962).

—, *John Milton: A Reader's Guide to His Poetry* (New York: Noonday Press, 1963).

North, Christopher R., *The Old Testament Interpretation of History* (London: Epworth Press, 1953).

Origen, *On First Principles*, translated and edited by G. W. Butterworth (London: SPCK, 1936).

O'Rourke, John J., "The Fulfillment Texts in Matthew", *Catholic Biblical Quarterly*, XXIV (1962), 394-403.

Patrides, C. A., "Milton and the Protestant Theory of Atonement", *PMLA*, LXXIV (1959), 7-13.

—, "The 'Protoevangelium' in Renaissance Theology and *Paradise Lost*", *SEL*, III, 19-30.

Patrizi, X., *Institutio De Interpretatione Librorum Bibliorum* (Rome, 1876).

Pecheux, Mother Mary Christopher, O.S.U., "The Concept of the Second Eve in *Paradise Lost*", *PMLA*, LXXV (1960), 359-366.

—, "Abraham, Adam and the Theme of Exile in *Paradise Lost*", *PMLA*, LXXX (1965), 365-371.

—, "The Second Adam and the Church in *Paradise Lost*", *The Journal of English Literary History*, XXXIV (1967), 173-187.

Pettet, E. C., *Of Paradise and Light: A Study of Vaughan's Silex Scintillans* (Cambridge: University Press, 1960).

Philo, Judeus, *Opera Omnia*, Tomus III (Lipsiae: Holtze, 1892).

Phythian-Adams, W. J., *The Fulness of Israel: A Study of the Meaning of Sacred History* (Oxford: University Press, 1938).

—, *The People and the Presence: A Study of the At-One-Ment* (Oxford: University Press, 1942).

—, *The Way of At-One-Ment* (Oxford: University Press, 1944).

van der Ploeg, J., O.P., "L'exégèse de l'Ancien Testament dans l'Épître aux Hebreux", *Revue Biblique*, LIV (1947), 187-228.

Pollard, A. W. and G. R. Redgrave, *A Short-Title Catalogue of Books Printed in England, Scotland, and Ireland, and of English Books Printed Abroad, 1475-1640* (London: The Bibliographical Society, 1946).

Pope, Elizabeth M., *Paradise Regained: The Tradition and the Poem* (New York: Russell and Russell, 1962).

Preiss, Theo, "The Christian Philosophy of History: The Vision of History in the New Testament", *The Journal of Religion*, XXX (1950), 157-170.

Prince, F. T., "On the Last Two Books of 'Paradise Lost'", *Essays and Studies*, XI (1958), 38-52.

Quasten, Johannes, *Patrology* (Westminster, Maryland: Newman Press, 1950).

Quesnell, Quentin, "Mary is the Church", *Thought*, XXXVI (1961), 25-39.

Quinn, Dennis B., "John Donne's Principles of Biblical Exegesis", *JEGP*, LXI (1962), 313-329.

—, "John Donne's Sermons on the Psalms and the Tradition of Biblical Exegesis", *Dissertation Abstracts*, XVIII (1958), 2131-2132.

von Rad, Gerhard, "Typological Interpretation of the Old Testament", *Interpretation*, XV (1961), 174-192.

Rahner, Hugo, S.J., *Our Lady and the Church*, translated by Sebastian Bullough, O.P. (New York: Pantheon Books, 1961).

Rahner, Karl, S.J., *Mary, Mother of the Lord* (New York, 1962).

Reiter, Robert Edward, "In Adam's Room. A Study of the Adamic Typology of Christ in *Paradise Regained*", *Dissertation Abstracts*, XXV (1964), 3581-3582.

Rice, W. G., *Paradise Regained* (= *Papers of the Michigan Academy of Science, Arts and Letters*, XXII).

Richardson, Alan, "The Rise of Modern Biblical Scholarship and Recent Discussions of the Authority of the Bible", *Cambridge History of the Bible*, 294-338.

Riesenfeld, Harald, *Jesus transfiguré* (København: Ejnar Munksgaard, 1947).

Robert, A. and A. Tricot, eds., *Initiation Biblique: Introduction a l'Etude des Saintes Ecritures*, troisième édition refondue (Paris: Desclée et Cie, 1954).

Robins, Harry F., *If This Be Heresy: A Study of Milton and Origen* (Urbana: University of Illinois Press, 1963).

Ross, M. M., *Poetry and Dogma: The Transfiguration of Eucharistic Symbols in Seventeenth Century Poetry* (New Brunswick: Rutgers University Press, 1954).

Røstvig, Maren-Sofie, "'Upon Appleton House' and the Universal History of Man", *English Studies*, XLII (1961).

Rowley, M. M., *The Re-Discovery of the Old Testament* (Philadelphia: The Westminster Press, 1946).

Rust, E. C., *The Christian Understanding of History* (London: Lutterworth Press, 1947).

Sablin, N., *Zur typologie des Johannes evangeliums* (1950).

Saint Andrew Bible Missal (Bruges, Belgium: Biblica, 1960).

Salter, K. W., *Thomas Traherne: Mystic and Poet* (London: Edward Arnold, Ltd., 1964).

Sandys, Edwin, *The Sermons*, edited for the Parker Society by Rev. John Ayre (Cambridge: At the University Press, 1841).

Schillebeeckx, E., *Marie, Mère de la Redemption* (Paris, 1963).

Schokel, Luis Alonzo, *Understanding Biblical Research* (New York: Herder and Herder, 1963).

Scott-Craig, T. S. K., "Concerning Milton's Samson", *Renaissance News*, V (1952), 43-53.

Semmelroth, O., *Urbild der Kirche* (Wurzburg, 1950).

Sims, James H., *The Bible in Milton's Epics* (Gainesville: University of Florida Press, 1962).

Smalley, Beryl, *The Study of the Bible in the Middle Ages* (Oxford: Basil Blackwell, 1952).

Smuts, J. C., *Holism and Evolution* (New York: The Macmillan Company, 1929).

Spenser, Edmund, *The Poems*, edited by J. C. Smith and E. De Selincourt (London: Oxford University Press, 1960).

Spicq, P. C., *Esquisse d'une Histoire de l'Exégèse Latine au Moyen Age* (Paris: J. Vrin, 1944).

Spitzer, Leo, "Marvell's 'Nymph Complaining for the Death of Her Faun': Sources Versus Meaning", *MLQ*, XIX (1958).

Stafford, Anthony, *The Femall Glory: or the life and Death of Our Blessed Lady, the Holy Virgin Mary, God's Owne Immaculate Mother* (1635).

Stambler, Elizabeth, "The Unity of Herbert's 'Temple'", *Cross Currents*, X (1960), 251-266.

Stapleton, Laurence, "Milton's Conception of Time in The Christian Doctrine", *Harvard Theological Review*, LVII (1964), 9-21.

Starkman, Miriam K., "Noble Numbers and the Poetry of Devotion", *Reason and the Imagination*, edited by Joseph A. Mazzeo (New York: Columbia University Press, 1962), 1-28.

Steadman, John M., "Bitter Ashes: Protestant Exegesis and the Serpent's Doom", *Studies in Philology*, LIX (1962), 201-210.

Steiner, M., *La tentation de Jesus dans l'interprétation patristique de Saint Justin à Origène*, Études Bibliques (Paris: J. Gabalda, 1962).

Summers, Joseph, "Herbert's Form", *PMLA*, LXVI (1951), 1055-1072.

—, *George Herbert: His Religion and Art* (Cambridge: Harvard University Press, 1954).

—, *The Muse's Method: An Introduction to Paradise Lost* (Cambridge: Harvard University Press, 1962).

Tasker, R. V. G., *The Old Testament in the New Testament* (London: SCM Press, Ltd., 1946).

Terrien, J. B., *La Mère de Dieu et la mère des hommes d'après les Pères et la théologie* (Paris, 1902).

Thils, G., "La théologie de l'histoire: note bibliographique", *Ephemerides Theologicae Lovanienses*, XXVI (1950), 87-95.

Tillyard, E. M. W., *Studies in Milton* (London: Chatto and Windus, 1951).

—, *The Elizabethan World Picture* (New York: Vintage Books, [no date]).

Traherne, Thomas, *Centuries, Poems and Thanksgivings*, edited by M. M. Margoliouth (Oxford: Clarendon Press, 1958).

Tresmontant, Claude, *A Study of Hebrew Thought*, translated by Michael Francis Gibson (New York: Desclée and Company, 1960).

Tromp, S., "Ecclesia Sponsa Virgo Mater", *Gregorianum*, XVIII (1937), 3-29.

Turner, H. E. W., *The Pattern of Christian Truth: a Study in the Relations Between Orthodoxy and Heresy* (Bampton Lectures, 1950) (London: A. R. Mowbray and Company, Ltd., 1954).

Tuve, Rosemond, "Imagery and Logic", *Journal of the History of Ideas*, III (1942), 374-400.

—, *A Reading of George Herbert* (Chicago: University of Chicago Press, 1952).

—, *Images and Themes in Five Poems of Milton* (1957).

—, *Allegorical Imagery* (Princeton: Princeton University Press, 1966).

de Tuya, Manuel, O.P., "El Sentido Tipico del Antigua Testamento es 'verdadera y estrictamento' sentido de la Biblia", *Ciencia Tomistica*, LXXX (1953).

Vaughan, Henry, *The Works*, edited by L. C. Martin, second edition (Oxford: Clarendon Press, 1957).

—, *A Comprehensive Bibliography*, edited by E. L. Marilla (= *University of Alabama Studies*, No. 3) (1948).

Venard, L., "Citations de l'Ancien Testament dans le Nouveau Testament", *Dictionnaire de la Bible. Supplement*, tome deuxième (1934), 23-51.

—, "Utilization de l'Ancien Testament dans le Nouveau", *Initiation Biblique*, edited by A. Robert and A. Tricot (Paris: Desclée et Cie. 1954), 446-450.

Walker, Fred, B., "Milton's Use of the Bible in His Shorter English Poems", Unpublished MA thesis, University of Florida, 1947.

Wallace, R. S., *Calvin's Doctrine of Word and Sacrament* (Edinburgh, 1953).

Wallerstein, Ruth C., *Richard Crashaw: A Study in Style and Poetic Development* (Madison: University of Wisconsin Press, 1959).

—, *Studies in Seventeenth-Century Poetic* (Madison: University of Wisconsin Press, 1950).

Walton, Isaak, *Lives of John Donne, Sir Henry Wotton, Richard Hooker, George Herbert and Robert Sanderson* (London: Oxford University Press, 1962).

Ward, Richard, *Theologicall questions, dogmaticall observations, and evangelicall essays, upon the gospel of Jesus Christ, according to St. Matthew* (London, 1640).

Warren, Austin, *Richard Crashaw: A Study in Baroque Sensibility* (Ann Arbor: University of Michigan Press, 1957).

Washbourne, Thomas, *Divine Poems*, London, 1654. Reprinted in the Fuller Worthies Library, edited by A. B. Grosart (London, 1868), Volume I.

Weemes, John, *The Christian Synagogue* (London, 1637).

Whatley, William, *Prototypes, or the primarie precedent presidents out of the book of Genesis. Showing, the good and bad things they did, and had, practically applied to our information and reformation* (London, 1640).

Whitaker, William, *A Disputation on Holy Scripture*, 1588, translated and edited for the Parker Society by Rev. William Fitzgerald (Cambridge: University Press, 1849).

White, Helen C., *English Devotional Literature, Prose: 1600-1640* (Madison: University of Wisconsin Press, 1931).

—, *The Tudor Books of Private Devotion* (Madison: University of Wisconsin Press, 1951).

—, *The Metaphysical Poets: A Study in Religious Experience* (New York: Collier Books, 1962).

White, Helen C., Ruth C. Wallerstein, and Ricardo Quintana, eds., *Seventeenth-Century Verse and Prose*, 2 volumes (New York: The Macmillan Company, 1959).

Willey, Basil, *The Seventeenth Century Background* (Garden City, New York: Doubleday and Company, 1953).

Williams, Arnold, "Renaissance Commentaries on Genesis and Some Elements of the Theology of *Paradise Lost*", *PMLA*, LVI (1941), 151-164.

—, *The Common Expositor: An Account of the Commentaries on Genesis, 1527-1633* (Chapel Hill: University of North Carolina Press, 1948).

Williams, George Walton, *Image and Symbol in the Sacred Poetry of Richard Crashaw* (Columbia: University of South Carolina Press).

Wilson, Elkin, *England's Eliza* (Cambridge: Harvard University Press, 1939).

Wing, Donald, ed., *Short-Title Catalogue of Books Printed in England, Scotland, Ireland, Wales and British America, and of English Books printed in other Countries, 1641-1700*, 3 vols. (New York: Columbia University Press, 1945).

Wolfson, Harry A., *The Philosophy of the Church Fathers* (Cambridge: Harvard University Press, 1956).

Wood, H. G., *Christianity and the Nature of History* (New York: Macmillan Company, 1934).

Woodhouse, A. S. P., "Some Notes on Milton's View of Creation", *PQ*, XXVIII (1949), 211-236.

Woollcombe, K. J., "Le sens de 'type' chez les Pères", *La vie spirituelle. Supplement*, tome IV (1951), 84-100.

—, "The Biblical Origins and Patristic Development of Typology", *Essays in Typology* (= *Studies in Biblical Theology*, 22) (Naperville, Illinois: Allenson, 1957), 39-75.

Zarb, Seraphin, O.P., "Unité ou Multiplicité des sens litteraux dans la Bible?", *Revue Thomiste*, XV (n.s.) (1932), 251-300.

INDEX